CONTENTS

Innovations

FROM JACK KILBY TO INTEL: A JOURNEY THROUGH THE HISTORY OF TRANSISTORS

Mark Spencer

ISBN:9798335903639

DEDICATION

To the visionaries and innovators who dared
to imagine a world transformed by technology.

And to my family, whose unwavering support
and encouragement have made this journey possible.

ACKNOWLEDGMENTS

Writing this book has been an incredible journey, one that would not have been possible without the support and contributions of many people.

First and foremost, I would like to express my deepest gratitude to my family—your love, encouragement, and patience have been the foundation upon which this book was built. Thank you for believing in me and for your understanding during the long hours of research and writing.

I am profoundly thankful to the pioneers of technology, especially Jack Kilby and the countless engineers and scientists whose work laid the groundwork for the modern world. Your ingenuity and perseverance continue to inspire and shape the future.

A special thank you to my colleagues and mentors in the field of engineering and technology history. Your insights, feedback, and shared enthusiasm have enriched this book beyond measure. I am particularly grateful to those who reviewed early drafts and provided valuable feedback—your suggestions helped refine and clarify my thoughts.

I would also like to acknowledge the many authors, historians, and technologists whose works I have studied over the years. Your research and publications have been instrumental in shaping my understanding of the history and impact of transistors.

Finally, to my readers—thank you for embarking on this journey with me. I hope this book provides you with not just a deeper understanding of the transistor's history, but also an appreciation for the technological marvels that continue to shape our world.

Thank you all for your support and encouragement. This book is as much yours as it is mine.

From Jack Kilby to Intel

A Journey through the History of Transistors

by Mark Spencer

PREFACE

My Journey with Transistors: From Curiosity to Transformation

For as long as I can remember, I've been captivated by the tiny miracles that power our world—transistors. These minuscule components have intrigued me not just for their technical brilliance but for the profound impact they have on every aspect of modern life. My journey began with a fascination for how things work, leading me to a career in engineering and a deep dive into the history of technological innovation. But it wasn't until I truly understood the transistor's role that I realized how much of our world is shaped by this small, yet mighty invention.

A World Before Transistors

To appreciate the marvel of the transistor, we must first step back in time. Imagine a world where the term "computer" referred to massive machines that filled entire rooms, powered by fragile and inefficient vacuum tubes. These tubes were the heart of early electronics, from radios to the first primitive computers. They were bulky, prone to failure, and consumed enormous amounts of power. The idea of portable electronics, or even something as commonplace today as a smartphone, was simply unthinkable.

In that era, technology was a luxury, available only to a few. The limitations of vacuum tubes meant that devices were large, expensive, and unreliable. Communication was slow, and the concept of a global, interconnected world was beyond the reach of even the most imaginative minds.

The Transistor Revolution: A Personal Perspective

My first encounter with a transistor was during my early days in engineering, and I was immediately struck by its elegance. Here was a device so small it could fit on the tip of your finger, yet it had the power to revolutionize everything from communication to computing. As I delved deeper into my studies and later into my career, I saw firsthand how transistors transformed the very fabric of our technological landscape.

The invention of the transistor in 1947 marked the beginning of a new era—one where technology could be both powerful and accessible. Suddenly, the world was no longer bound by the constraints of bulky vacuum tubes. Radios became pocket-sized, computers began to shrink from room-filling giants to something more manageable, and entirely new industries began to emerge. The transistor didn't just improve existing technology; it made possible the digital revolution that followed.

As someone who has spent years researching and working with cutting-edge technologies, I've seen the incredible evolution of the transistor up close. I've had the privilege of watching microprocessors—those complex chips packed with billions of transistors—become the brains behind everything from our laptops to our cars. The transistor's journey from an experimental device to the cornerstone of modern electronics is nothing short of awe-inspiring.

The Future Beckons

Looking ahead, the future of transistors holds even greater promise. As we push the limits of Moore's Law, the traditional silicon-based transistor is nearing its physical boundaries. Yet, the field is far from stagnant. Researchers are exploring new frontiers, from quantum transistors to materials like graphene that could usher in a new era of speed and efficiency. These advancements could redefine computing, opening doors to possibilities we can scarcely imagine today.

As someone who has been deeply involved in the world of technology, I am both excited and optimistic about what lies ahead. The transistor, once a humble invention, continues to be the foundation upon which we build our future. It's a testament to human ingenuity and the relentless pursuit of progress.

In this book, I invite you to join me on a journey through the history of the transistor. Together, we'll explore its origins, its evolution, and its far-reaching impact on our world. We'll also look ahead to the future, where the transistor will continue to be at the heart of groundbreaking innovations that will shape the next chapter of our technological story.

As we embark on this journey, I hope to share not just the story of the transistor, but also my passion for the technology that drives our world forward. I believe that by understanding where we've come from, we can better appreciate the incredible possibilities that lie ahead.

Welcome to the world of the transistor—where the smallest components have the power to change everything.

CHAPTER 1: THE BIRTH OF THE TRANSISTOR

F ew inventions in the realm of technological advancements have revolutionized the world as profoundly as the transistor. It is a testament to human ingenuity and a landmark moment in the history of technology. Leading the way in this journey is Jack Kilby, the pioneering mind behind one of the most impactful inventions of the 20th century.

The year was 1947 when the world was on the cusp of a technological renaissance. Major breakthroughs were imminent, but the electronic landscape of that time faced a big challenge— a reliance on bulky vacuum tubes. These tubes consumed substantial power and were prone to failure, hindering progress in a world where miniaturization was the key to success.

In this context, Kilby, a physicist and electrical engineer, embarked on a mission to find a solution. Fresh out of the University of Illinois, he commenced his career at Bell Labs, a hotbed of scientific research.

Kilby's innovative breakthrough unfolded on a scorching summer day in 1958, with the relentless Texas sun casting a golden hue over his makeshift lab. Seeking a way to eliminate the complicated web of wires and intricate parts that plagued electronic circuits, he had a radical idea: What if he could create an all-in-one device, small enough to fit in the palm of a hand, without compromising functionality? This brilliant idea inspired him to create what is now known as an integrated circuit.

In a David vs. Goliath scenario, Kilby embarked on an audacious endeavor to turn his vision into reality. Working tirelessly in his makeshift lab, armed with a shoestring budget, he managed to successfully demonstrate his invention to the world just a year later, in 1959.

Kilby's revolutionary integrated circuit, which he affectionately called "the Solid Circuit," marked a pivotal moment that would change the course of history. Comprised of a small piece of germanium with three tiny wires meticulously attached, it was a triumph of simplicity and elegance. This humble creation would pave the way for the birth of the transistor—an innovation that would shape the future of technology.

At its core, the transistor symbolized a monumental leap in electronic engineering. Gone were the days of bulky vacuum tubes; the transistor offered unparalleled miniaturization, enhanced performance, and increased reliability. Kilby's invention opened up a world of possibilities, enabling the creation of smaller, faster, and more efficient electronic devices than ever before.

The rapid adoption of transistors unleashed a wave of advancements across various industries. From the realm of telecommunications to computing, these tiny yet powerful devices played a transformational role. They fueled the development of smaller and more portable radios, led to the emergence of the first mainframe computers, and even found their way into critical space missions.

But perhaps one of the greatest impacts of Kilby's invention lay in its democratizing effect on technology. The transistor revolutionized consumer electronics, making previously expensive items like televisions and radios affordable and ubiquitous in households worldwide. The once-unattainable dream of having a television set or a personal computer became a reality for households around the world.

Kilby's innovative breakthrough not only disrupted the technological landscape but also sparked a chain reaction of progress. It laid the groundwork for the birth of Intel Corporation in 1968, a company that would become synonymous with advancements in the semiconductor industry.

Contemplating Jack Kilby's extraordinary feat and the dawn of the transistor, one cannot help but envision the boundless horizons of innovation waiting to be explored. The impact of this groundbreaking invention reverberates in every aspect of our lives, acting as a catalyst for innovation on a global scale.

Indeed, the journey from Kilby's ingenuity to the transformative power of the transistor is an awe-inspiring testament to human curiosity and perseverance. As the next chapter of this riveting tale awaits, let us venture deeper into the annals of history, where unprecedented technological wonders await us. And so, the story continues...With the birth of the transistor, the world stood at the precipice of a technological revolution. Kilby's groundbreaking invention opened up a world of possibilities, inspiring an era of innovation that would shape the future of technology as we know it.

The global scientific community eagerly embraced Kilby's revolutionary integrated circuit as news of its impact spread worldwide. The transistor's unparalleled miniaturization, enhanced performance, and increased reliability sparked a transformative wave of advancements in telecommunications, computing, and aerospace industries, reshaping the technological landscape.

In the realm of telecommunications, the transistor played a pivotal role. The once-bulky and cumbersome telephone systems were gradually replaced with compact and efficient devices. Transistors enabled the development of smaller, lighter, and more reliable telephones, making communication faster and more accessible than ever before. The transistor's impact reverberated worldwide, enabling real-time communication through satellite technology and undersea cables, revolutionizing how people connect across continents.

The computing industry also experienced a profound transformation thanks to Kilby's invention. Gone were the days of room-sized computers that required immense power and took up entire floors. With the integration of transistors, computers became smaller, faster, and more reliable. This newfound efficiency led to the emergence of the first mainframe computers, which revolutionized data processing and opened the door to the digital age.

Moreover, the transistor found its way into critical space missions, where its reliability and miniaturization were paramount. Kilby's revolutionary invention propelled technological advancements in aerospace exploration, powering the computers and communication systems vital for manned space missions. With the transistor's help, humanity reached for the stars, expanding our understanding of the universe and setting the stage for future interstellar endeavors.

However, perhaps one of the most remarkable aspects of Kilby's invention was its democratizing effect on technology. The transistor brought consumer electronics to the masses, making them accessible to a broader audience. The days of expensive and scarce television sets and personal computers were replaced with affordable and widely available devices. Kilby's invention turned the once-unattainable dream into a reality for households around the world, empowering individuals and communities with the tools to connect, learn, and grow.

The impact of Kilby's invention extended beyond individual devices and ignited a revolution in the semiconductor industry. It provided the foundation for the birth of Intel Corporation in 1968, a company that would go on to become a global leader in semiconductor manufacturing. Intel's relentless pursuit of innovation and technological advancement owes its origins to the transformative power of the transistor, solidifying its place in the annals of technology history.

As we reflect upon the journey from Kilby's ingenuity to the far-reaching impact of the transistor, we are reminded of the infinite possibilities that lie ahead. Today, as we stand on the brink of the Fourth Industrial Revolution, the transistor continues to be the bedrock upon which our technological advancements are built. It is the catalyst that fuels innovation, propelling us forward into an era of artificial intelligence, quantum computing, and unimaginable breakthroughs.

In conclusion, the birth of the transistor was a defining moment in human history. It sparked a chain reaction of progress, transformed industries, and empowered individuals worldwide. From the humble beginnings of Kilby's makeshift lab to the global impact felt across all facets of society, the transistor stands as an enduring symbol of human curiosity and perseverance. As we embark on the next chapter of technological marvels, let us draw inspiration from the legacy of Kilby and the transformative power of the transistor. The possibilities are endless, waiting to be discovered and unleashed. And so, the story continues, and the world marches forward into a future shaped by the revolutionary birth of the transistor.

CHAPTER 2: EARLY DEVELOPMENTS IN TRANSISTOR TECHNOLOGY

I n the ever-evolving world of technology, certain breakthroughs have proven to be pivotal moments that shape the course of history. One such milestone is the invention of the transistor, which revolutionized the electronics industry and propelled human innovation to unprecedented heights. To truly appreciate the significance of transistors in our lives today, we must delve into the early advancements and inventions that paved the way for their widespread use in various applications.

The roots of transistor technology can

be traced back to the mid-20th century when scientists and engineers began exploring alternatives to the existing vacuum tube technology. These massive, delicate, and power-hungry devices were the building blocks of early electronic systems but had limitations that hindered their potential. Enter the transistor, a small and efficient semiconductor device capable of amplifying and switching electronic signals.

One of the key players in the development of transistors was Jack Kilby. In 1958, Kilby, working at Texas Instruments, made a groundbreaking discovery that would forever change the world of electronics. He successfully integrated several electronic components onto a small piece of germanium, creating the first integrated circuit (IC). This breakthrough laid the foundation for the miniaturization of electronic devices, eventually leading to the birth of modern computers, smartphones, and countless other gadgets we rely on today.

However, Kilby's invention was not the first attempt at creating a solid-state electronic device to replace vacuum tubes. In the early 1940s, a trio of scientists consisting of Walter Brattain, John Bardeen, and William Shockley were working at Bell Labs in the United States. Their collaboration resulted in the invention of the point-contact transistor, which led to them being awarded the Nobel Prize in Physics in 1956. This transistor represented a major advancement, as it was more reliable, compact, and consumed less power than its predecessors.

Building upon the point-contact transistor, Shockley, in collaboration with his team, subsequently introduced the junction transistor in 1951. This type of transistor was not only more reliable but also exhibited better performance characteristics, making it commercially viable. The junction transistor comprised multiple layers of semiconductor material, forming junctions with distinct properties that controlled the flow of electric current. This increased control over the flow of electrons opened up endless possibilities for future technological advancements.

As the pursuit of improved transistor technology continued, luminaries like Gordon Teal at Texas Instruments and William Shockley at Bell Labs made groundbreaking contributions, propelling the field forward with their innovative discoveries. In 1953, Gordon Teal at Texas Instruments developed the grown-junction transistor, which utilized a chemical process to create p-n junctions in silicon – a material that would later dominate the industry due to its abundance and desirable properties. Teal's invention significantly improved the reliability and manufacturing scalability of transistors, setting the stage for their mass production.

The advancements in transistor technology

during this period were accompanied by a surge in applications across various industries. Transistors found their way into telephony, radios, and early computers. Their small size, low power consumption, and improved performance made them an ideal solution for these devices. Suddenly, the world was witnessing the birth of portable radios, smaller televisions, and the dawn of the digital age.

As the first half of this chapter draws to a close, we've explored the early developments that paved the way for the widespread use of transistors. The evolution from the point-contact transistor to the junction transistor marked significant milestones in the journey towards the compact, efficient, and reliable transistors we depend on today. In the next part of this chapter, we will continue on this exciting journey, unraveling the transformative role of transistors in the growth of computing power, communication systems, and beyond. Stay tuned, for the story is nowhere near its conclusion.

As we continue our journey through the history of transistor technology, we dive deeper into the transformative role transistors played in the growth of computing power, communication systems, and beyond. These remarkable inventions have reshaped our world by enabling the proliferation of smartphones, the automation of industries, and the seamless connectivity of global networks, propelling us into an era defined by innovation and interconnectedness.

In the late 1950s and early 1960s, transistors began to replace vacuum tubes in electronic systems, leading to the development of remarkable inventions that shaped the future. One such breakthrough was the introduction of the first commercially available transistor radio in 1954 by Texas Instruments. This pocket-sized device captured the imagination of consumers worldwide and represented a major shift in how people could experience entertainment on-the-go. Suddenly, music and news became portable, setting the stage for a revolution in personal electronics.

The proliferation of transistors also presented new possibilities in the field of computing. In 1959, the IBM 1401 became the first transistorized computer, marking a significant milestone in the history of computing. This breakthrough not only reduced the size of computers but also made them more reliable and energy-efficient. With transistors at its core, the IBM 1401 and subsequent models revolutionized business and scientific computing, making complex tasks more accessible to a wider audience.

The advancements in transistor technology continued to drive innovation in the telecommunications industry as well. In the early

1960s, transistors found their way into the first touch-tone telephones, replacing the bulky rotary dial systems. This development not only enhanced the speed and efficiency of telephone communication but also laid the groundwork for the future integration of telephony with digital technologies.

The miniaturization and increased performance of transistors also enabled the development of early electronic calculators. In 1967, Texas Instruments introduced the first handheld electronic calculator, the TI-2500. This device marked a significant leap forward in computational capabilities and made complex mathematical calculations accessible to individuals and professionals alike. The integration of transistors into calculators revolutionized computational capabilities, transforming these devices from basic arithmetic tools to sophisticated computing machines that laid the foundation for modern computing.

Moreover, transistors played a crucial role in the advent of integrated circuits (ICs) – a technological marvel that further revolutionized the electronics industry. The shrinking size and increased capabilities of transistors made it possible to fit thousands, and later millions, of them onto a single silicon chip. This breakthrough enabled the creation of more sophisticated and powerful electronic systems, including computers, smartphones, and other portable devices that we depend on today.

The impact of transistors on society cannot be overstated. They have accelerated the pace of technological development and opened up avenues of innovation that were previously unimaginable. From the early point-contact transistor to the development of integrated circuits, each milestone built upon the previous one, fueling a continuous cycle of progress.

Looking to the future, researchers and engineers are exploring the potential of new transistor technologies, such as carbon nanotube transistors and quantum transistors, that could lead to further advancements in computing power, energy efficiency, and data storage.

As we reach the end of this chapter, we stand in awe of the remarkable journey from the early developments in transistor technology to the sophisticated electronic systems that dominate our world today. Transistors have not only changed the way we live, work, and communicate but have also created a solid foundation for future technological advancements. Let us remember and celebrate the pioneers who paved the way for this transformative technology, and embrace the endless possibilities that lie ahead.

CHAPTER 3:
THE RISE OF
INTEGRATED
CIRCUITS

I n the early days of electronic devices, a remarkable development took place that would forever change the course of technology. It was the birth of integrated circuits, a revolutionary advancement that would lead to the miniaturization and enhanced functionality of electronic components. In this chapter, we will delve into the emergence of integrated circuits and explore how they transformed the capabilities of electronic devices.

To truly understand the significance of integrated circuits, we must first recognize the pivotal role played by Jack Kilby, the brilliant engineer credited with their invention. In 1958, Kilby, then working at Texas Instruments, had an innovative idea that would bring together multiple electronic components onto a single semiconductor material. This groundbreaking concept laid the foundation for what we know today as integrated circuits.

Kilby's invention paved the way for the manufacturing of complex electronic devices that could outperform their predecessors. By combining transistors, resistors, and capacitors onto a single chip, the integrated circuit enabled significant advancements in both size and performance. This leap in technology was driven by the inherent advantages of these microelectronic wonders.

One of the key advantages of integrated circuits was their ability to greatly reduce the size of electronic devices. Before their introduction, electronic circuits were composed of numerous bulky individual components. Imagine a room filled with vacuum tubes and wires, each serving a specific function. These large and complicated assemblies were not only cumbersome but also limited the scope of technological innovation.

With the arrival of integrated circuits, the landscape of electronics changed dramatically. The compact size of these circuits allowed for the development of smaller, portable devices that could be easily carried and used in various settings. As the size decreased, the capabilities of these devices increased exponentially, opening a world of possibilities for technological advancements.

Beyond their size reduction, integrated circuits brought about a significant improvement in the performance and functionality of electronic devices. By integrating various components onto a single chip, the connections between them became shorter and faster. This led to increased speed, efficiency, and reliability, making way for the development of more powerful devices that could handle complex tasks with precision.

Moreover, integrated circuits facilitated the integration of multiple functions within a single device. No longer limited to performing one specific task, electronic devices could now house multiple functionalities. For instance, calculators evolved from bulky devices with limited capabilities to sleek pocket-sized gadgets capable of performing complex mathematical calculations.

The incredible impact of integrated circuits extended beyond calculators, revolutionizing numerous industries. From telecommunications to automotive, aerospace to medical, the application of integrated circuits permeated every aspect of modern life. The digital revolution would not have been possible without these miniature technological marvels.

As we delve deeper into the second half of this chapter, we will explore how integrated circuits continued to evolve and shape the world of electronics. The dawn of microprocessors and the integration of millions of transistors onto a single chip would catapult technology to even greater heights, fueling innovation and transforming the way we live and work.

And just as the pioneers of integrated circuits pushed the boundaries of innovation, the story of their rise is far from over. Our exploration of their impact on technology has only just begun. Join us in the next part of this chapter as we uncover the fascinating developments that lay ahead, waiting to change the course of history once more.In the second half of the chapter, we will continue our exploration of the evolution and impact of integrated circuits. Building upon the groundbreaking advancements made by Jack Kilby and his invention, the integrated circuit, technology enthusiasts witnessed a series of remarkable developments that propelled the world of electronics even further.

As the demand for smaller and more powerful devices continued to grow, engineers faced the challenge of fitting even more components onto a single chip. This led to the next monumental breakthrough in the history of integrated circuits - the birth of microprocessors. These tiny computational powerhouses paved the way for the digital age and revolutionized the capabilities of electronic devices.

In 1971, Intel introduced the world's first commercially available microprocessor, the Intel 4004. This single chip contained a staggering 2,300 transistors, exponentially more than the integrated circuits of the past. The microprocessor marked a major turning point, as it not only integrated multiple electronic components but also included a central processing unit (CPU) on the chip itself, enabling it to execute complex instructions and calculations.

The advent of microprocessors opened up

new possibilities for the development of personal computers (PCs). Over the years, continuous advancements in microprocessor technology led to increasingly powerful and efficient CPUs. The rapid growth of processing power and the ability to handle complex tasks laid the foundation for the modern computing landscape.

With the introduction of microprocessors, electronic devices became more versatile and capable of performing a wide range of functions. From desktop computers to laptops, smartphones to smartwatches, the integration of microprocessors allowed for the convergence of technologies, enabling one device to handle multiple tasks seamlessly.

Moreover, the integration of millions, and later billions, of transistors onto a single chip enabled the creation of high-performance digital systems. Through the concept of Very Large Scale Integration (VLSI), the industry managed to shrink transistor size while increasing their numbers, ultimately achieving incredible levels of computational power.

The relentless pursuit of miniaturization and increased performance led to the development of System-on-Chip (SoC) technology, where all the necessary components of a complete system are integrated onto a single chip. SoCs, commonly found in smartphones and other portable electronic devices, combine computational power, memory, communication capabilities, and various other functionalities into one compact package.

The impact of integrated circuits and microprocessors extended far beyond the realms of personal computing. These advancements sparked significant progress in fields such as telecommunications, aerospace, and medicine. The integration of increasingly powerful and reliable chips enabled the creation of sophisticated communication networks, revolutionizing global connectivity. Satellites, aircraft, and medical devices all benefited from the miniaturization and enhanced functionality provided by integrated circuits.

Beyond their immediate practical applications, integrated circuits and microprocessors have fundamentally transformed society on a broader scale. The digital age, driven by these technological marvels, has ushered in a new era of information access, connectivity, and innovation. The world has become more interconnected than ever before, with data flowing seamlessly through networks and devices to drive societal and economic advancements.

In conclusion, the rise of integrated circuits and microprocessors has had a profound impact on the world of technology. Through the ingenuity of pioneers like Jack Kilby and the continuous efforts of engineers and researchers, these miniature technological marvels have transformed the capabilities of electronic devices, revolutionized industries, and shaped the way we live and work. The journey is far from over, as the continued advancements in integrated circuit technology promise even greater possibilities and advancements yet to come. Stay tuned as we venture forth into the future, where the boundaries of innovation continue to be pushed, and the world of transistors continues to evolve.

CHAPTER 4: THE BIRTH OF INTEL CORPORATION

T he founding of Intel Corporation stands as one such moment, forever altering the landscape of the transistor industry. Its inception marked a turning point, propelling the growth and diffusion of transistor technology to unprecedented levels. In this chapter, we delve into the intriguing journey that led to the birth of Intel Corporation and its profound impact on the world.

To truly grasp the significance of Intel's founding, it is essential to first revisit the humble origins of the transistor itself. The transistor, a fundamental building block of modern electronics, was first invented by Jack Kilby. His pioneering work in the late 1950s led to the development of the integrated circuit, a revolutionary technology that brought together multiple transistors on a single chip. This breakthrough opened up new possibilities in the world of computing and laid the groundwork for Intel's future.

It was in the year 1968 that the transformative event took place. Robert Noyce, a brilliant engineer known for his co-invention of the integrated circuit, joined forces with Gordon Moore, another visionary in the field. Together, they embarked on a mission to establish a new company that would redefine the boundaries of the semiconductor industry. With the invaluable support of Arthur Rock, a venture capitalist, the groundwork for Intel Corporation was laid.

At its inception, Intel's primary focus was on the production of semiconductor memory chips. The market at the time was dominated by Japanese manufacturers, posing a challenge for Intel due to intense competition and established market presence. However, with the exceptional leadership of Noyce and Moore, and their unwavering belief in innovation, Intel managed to break through the barriers.

One of the key strategies that set Intel apart was their commitment to research and development. They recognized that to stay ahead of the competition, they needed to constantly push the boundaries of what was possible. This emphasis on technological advancement led to the creation of groundbreaking products, such as the Intel 1103, the world's first commercially available dynamic random-access memory (DRAM) chip.

The launch of the Intel 1103 in 1970 propelled Intel into the spotlight, firmly establishing the company as a force to be reckoned with. Its success not only solidified Intel's position in the semiconductor industry but also set the stage for their future endeavors. Building on this momentum, Intel went on to introduce a series of influential products, each pushing the boundaries of technology further.

As Intel continued to revolutionize the semiconductor landscape, the company faced its fair share of challenges. The constant need to innovate and adapt in a rapidly evolving industry put Intel's capabilities to the test. However, time and time again, they demonstrated their resilience and ability to overcome obstacles. The journey of Intel Corporation has been one of perseverance, passion, and an unwavering dedication to technological advancements.

Pausing at this juncture in our narrative, we witness Intel Corporation on the verge of a new era. Their relentless pursuit of innovation has brought them to the forefront of the semiconductor industry, with their influence reaching far beyond the realm of transistors. The impact of Intel's groundbreaking technologies can be felt in every facet of our lives, from the devices we use daily to the infrastructures that power the world.

In the second half of this chapter, we will delve deeper into Intel's continued growth, exploring their contributions to the evolution of transistor technology and their role as a catalyst for change in the global landscape. So, join us as we embark on the second phase of this captivating journey, where Intel's story unfolds further, revealing the interplay between technology, ambition, and the relentless pursuit of progress.With the founding of Intel Corporation, the semiconductor industry was forever altered, setting off a chain of events that would revolutionize technology as we know it. In the first half of this chapter, we explored the humble origins of the transistor and the early milestones that laid the foundation for Intel's future. Now, let us delve into the second half of Intel's journey and unravel the interconnected web of innovation, progress, and transformation.

As Intel gained momentum in the late 1970s, it became evident that their commitment to research and development was a driving force behind their success. One of their most groundbreaking advancements during this period was the development of the x86 architecture, which would become the cornerstone of modern computing. The Intel 8086 processor, released in 1978, marked a significant milestone in the evolution of microprocessors, heralding the era of personal computing.

The PC revolution took off in earnest with the introduction of the IBM Personal Computer (PC) in 1981, which was powered by Intel's 8088 processor. Intel continued to innovate, releasing the 80286 processor in 1982 and the 80386 in 1985, which significantly increased computing power and laid the groundwork for the graphical user interfaces we use today. These advancements in processor technology fueled the rapid growth of the PC industry, democratizing access to computing and transforming the way we work, communicate, and entertain ourselves.

Throughout the 1990s, Intel solidified its position as a global technology giant. The release of the Pentium processor in 1993 marked another significant leap forward in computing power, cementing Intel's dominance in the market. As the demand for faster and more efficient processors increased, Intel continued to deliver, introducing new iterations of the Pentium series and pioneering the concept of Moore's Law.

Moore's Law, postulated by Intel co-founder Gordon Moore, stated that the number of transistors on a microchip would double approximately every two years. This prediction became a driving force behind Intel's relentless pursuit of innovation, challenging their engineers to constantly push the boundaries of what was possible. The advent of the Pentium Pro processor in 1995 showcased the company's unwavering commitment to Moore's Law, delivering unprecedented processing power and solidifying Intel's reputation as a leader in semiconductor technology.

As the new millennium dawned, Intel faced new challenges brought about by the rise of mobile computing and the internet. The company keenly recognized the shifting landscape and embarked on a diversification strategy to adapt to evolving consumer needs. With the introduction of the Centrino platform in 2003, Intel revolutionized mobile computing, optimizing power efficiency and wireless connectivity.

Innovation at Intel extended beyond processors and microchips. The company made significant investments in emerging technologies such as artificial intelligence, machine learning, and the Internet of Things (IoT). Intel's ability to stay ahead of the curve has enabled them to play a pivotal role in shaping the future of technology, from autonomous vehicles to smart cities.

Today, Intel continues to be at the forefront of technological advancements, driving innovation in fields such as quantum computing, neuromorphic computing, and high-performance computing. The company's commitment to research and development remains unwavering, fostering collaborations with industry partners, universities, and research institutions worldwide.

Intel Corporation's compelling journey, characterized by overcoming industry challenges, pioneering innovative breakthroughs, and demonstrating unwavering dedication to technological progress, stands as a testament to their resilience and passion. From the transistor's humble origins to the integrated circuit's world-changing impact, Intel's story showcases the transformative power of innovation and collective human effort.

As we conclude this chapter, we invite you to reflect on the remarkable journey Intel has undertaken, continuously pushing the boundaries of what is possible in the realm of transistor technology. The founding of Intel Corporation and its subsequent achievements have paved the way for a future where technological advancements permeate every aspect of our lives, elevating humanity's potential to new heights. Intel's story is far from over, and with each passing day, the company continues to redefine what is possible, inspiring generations of technology enthusiasts to dream big and embrace the relentless pursuit of progress.

CHAPTER 5: THE EVOLUTION OF TRANSISTOR SIZES

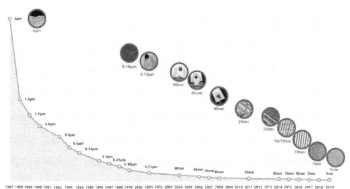

I n the ever-evolving world of technology, size matters. Exploring the captivating history of transistors reveals that their ongoing miniaturization has significantly contributed to the rapid technological advancements we observe today. Reducing the size of these essential components of modern electronics has greatly affected how devices perform, consume power, and advance technologically.

To fully grasp the significance of transistor size reduction, we need to travel back in time to the origins of this remarkable invention. Jack Kilby, one of the key figures in the field of transistor development, revolutionized electronics with the invention of the integrated circuit (IC) at Texas Instruments in 1958. Kilby's groundbreaking work opened up a world of possibilities, allowing multiple transistors to be fabricated on a single chip of semiconductor material.

At the birth of integrated circuits, transistors were relatively large compared to their contemporary counterparts. These early transistors were constructed using bulky discrete components that required sizable real estate on a circuit board. However, As researchers and engineers explored the complexities of these small devices further, they quickly recognized the potential for substantial improvements through miniaturization.

Throughout the 1960s and 1970s, enormous strides were made in shrinking the size of transistors. The driving force behind this advancement was Moore's Law, coined by Intel co-founder Gordon Moore in 1965. Moore's Law observed that the number of transistors on a chip would double approximately every two years. This forecast has been remarkably precise and has driven the semiconductor industry's dedicated efforts to create smaller, more effective transistors.

The progressive miniaturization of transistors led to numerous technological breakthroughs. Smaller transistors meant that more of them could be packed onto a single chip, resulting in increased computing power. This phenomenon led to the development of ever more powerful and capable computers, paving the way for a digital revolution that has transformed every aspect of our lives.

As the size of transistors decreased, so too did their power consumption. The advancements in transistor size reduction directly contributed to the rise of portable electronics. Devices we now take for granted, such as smartphones and tablets, would not have been possible without the ability to manufacture smaller, energy-efficient transistors. The miniaturization of transistors enabled electronics to become more portable, fueling a new era of connectivity and accessibility.

Moreover, smaller transistors not only improved power efficiency but also led to significant improvements in overall device performance. With each reduction in size, transistors became faster and more reliable, enabling the development of high-performance processors and cutting-edge applications. These progressions drove advancements in industries spanning from artificial intelligence to healthcare, empowering scientists, engineers, and researchers to explore new horizons and drive innovation.

The journey from the early, large-scale transistor designs to the ultra-small transistors we see today has been nothing short of extraordinary. However, the evolution of transistor sizes did not come without its challenges. As we venture further into this chapter, we will explore the obstacles encountered along the way, such as quantum effects, and how scientists and engineers overcame these hurdles to continue the incredible march toward smaller transistors.

Stay tuned for the second half of this chapter where we delve deeper into the fascinating world of transistor miniaturization. We will uncover the current state of transistor sizes, the cutting-edge technologies and techniques used in their manufacturing, and the future prospects of this ongoing journey toward ever-smaller and more efficient transistors. The next part promises to be an exciting exploration of the present and future of this crucial technological advancement.As we continue our exploration of the fascinating world of transistor miniaturization, we delve into the current state of transistor sizes and the cutting-edge technologies and techniques used in their manufacturing. The continuous effort to create smaller and more efficient transistors has led us to the current state of technology and holds promise for a future brimming with possibilities.

In recent years, transistor sizes have reached astonishingly small scales, with current transistors measuring in the nanometer range. Today, the most advanced processors are built using transistor sizes as small as 5 nanometers, enabling unprecedented levels of performance and power efficiency. For context, a single nanometer is approximately 100,000 times thinner than the width of a human hair. This high degree of accuracy in manufacturing serves as evidence of the remarkable advancements achieved in semiconductor technology.

The manufacturing process for these ultra-small transistors involves intricate techniques, such as photolithography and atomic layer deposition. Photolithography is a process that uses light to transfer a pattern onto a semiconductor wafer, allowing for the precise placement of transistor components. Atomic layer deposition, on the other hand, involves depositing thin layers of materials atom by atom, ensuring the utmost precision in the construction of transistors.

One of the major challenges that arise with shrinking transistor sizes to such extremes is the impact of quantum effects. At these minuscule scales, quantum mechanics comes into play, causing phenomena that must be carefully controlled and mitigated. For instance, quantum tunneling occurs when electrons can pass through traditionally insulating materials, leading to current leakage and reduced overall device reliability. To combat this, engineers have employed innovative solutions, such as incorporating new materials and introducing intricate transistor designs that minimize the effects of quantum tunneling.

Another significant challenge is the growing complexity and cost associated with developing and manufacturing these ultra-small transistors. As transistor sizes continue to decrease, the number of transistors that can be packed onto a chip increases exponentially. This exponential growth in transistor count poses difficulties in chip design, circuit integration, and heat dissipation. Additionally, the cost of building state-of-the-art fabrication facilities that can handle the intricate manufacturing processes involved becomes increasingly prohibitive. These challenges require constant innovation and collaboration between researchers, engineers, and the semiconductor industry as a whole.

Looking forward, the future of transistor miniaturization holds exciting prospects. Beyond the current state of 5 nanometers, researchers are already exploring the development of transistors measuring just a few atoms wide. These advancements are not only limited to traditional silicon-based transistors but also extend to novel materials and technologies, such as graphene and carbon nanotubes. These alternative materials have the potential to revolutionize the way we think about transistor design and enable even smaller and more efficient devices.

Furthermore, researchers are investigating alternative computing paradigms that can harness the power of quantum mechanics. Quantum computing, still in its infancy, promises to usher in a new era of computing power, where computations are performed using quantum bits, or qubits. While quantum computers are currently limited to a small number of qubits and face technical challenges, they offer the potential for incredibly fast and efficient processing that could revolutionize fields such as cryptography, optimization, and drug discovery.

In conclusion, the evolution of transistor sizes has been a remarkable journey driven by the relentless pursuit of smaller, more efficient, and more powerful devices. From the groundbreaking invention of the integrated circuit by Jack Kilby to the current state-of-the-art nanoscale transistors, the miniaturization of transistors has fueled technological advancements across various industries. Despite the challenges posed by quantum effects and escalating manufacturing complexities, the future of transistor miniaturization holds immense promise. As technology enthusiasts, we eagerly await the next breakthroughs that will continue to shape and transform our world.

CHAPTER 6: TRANSISTOR APPLICATIONS IN COMMUNICATIO N SYSTEMS

The history of transistors is intricately intertwined with the development of communication systems. These tiny semiconductor devices revolutionized the way we communicate, enabling the creation of devices like radios, televisions, and phones that have become an integral part of our daily lives. Let us embark on a journey through time to discover how transistors transformed the world of communication.

Before the advent of transistors, communication systems heavily relied on vacuum tubes. While these vacuum tubes paved the way for important advancements, they were bulky, power-hungry, and prone to overheating. This limited their potential for widespread application in communication devices. However, all that changed with the groundbreaking invention of the transistor by Jack Kilby.

Jack Kilby, an engineer at Texas Instruments, is credited with the invention of the first integrated circuit, which included the transistor. He successfully demonstrated his invention in 1958, showing the world a glimpse of the future of communication systems. Suddenly, electronic devices were no longer bound by the limitations of vacuum tubes.

The transistor, a small device made of semiconductor material such as silicon or germanium, acts as an amplifier and a switch. Its ability to amplify electrical signals and control the flow of current made it a game-changer in communication systems. By manipulating the properties of transistors, engineers were able to miniaturize electronic devices, reduce power consumption, and enhance overall performance.

One of the first practical applications of transistors was in the field of radios. With transistors replacing vacuum tubes, radios became smaller, cheaper, and more portable. This shift paved the way for the transistor radio, a revolutionary device that allowed people to carry their favorite tunes with them wherever they went. The transistor radio became an icon of the 1960s, empowering individuals with the ability to access news, music, and entertainment on the move.

The impact of transistors extended beyond radios. Television sets, which were previously bulky and limited to a few channels, underwent a remarkable transformation. The integration of transistors led to the development of portable televisions and introduced the concept of remote controls. Televisions became more accessible, allowing people to enjoy their favorite shows from the comfort of their homes.

Phones also experienced a major revolution thanks to transistors. The introduction of the transistor provided phones with greater efficiency, improved sound quality, and reduced costs. The transition from rotary dial phones to touchtone phones, with the integration of transistors and their switching capabilities, made communication more convenient and efficient.

Moreover, transistors played a crucial role in the development of mobile communication systems. With the invention of the first cellular phone by Martin Cooper in 1973, the world witnessed a new era of wireless communication. Transistors enabled the miniaturization of mobile devices, making them portable and accessible to a wider audience. As the capabilities of transistors advanced, so did the evolution of mobile phones, leading to the smartphones we rely on today for countless communication and digital tasks.

The first half of this chapter has taken us on a remarkable journey through the applications of transistors in communication systems. From the groundbreaking invention by Jack Kilby to the miniaturization of radios, televisions, and phones, transistors have transformed the way we communicate and connect with the world around us.

But this is just the beginning. The second half of this chapter delves deeper into the impact of transistors, exploring their role in satellite communication, internet connectivity, and the future of communication systems. Prepare yourself to uncover the astonishing possibilities that lay ahead as we continue our exploration in the second part of this chapter.

Stay tuned – the power of transistors in communication systems is about to unfold in ways you never imagined.The Impact of Transistors in Satellite Communication Systems

Having explored the transformative applications of transistors in radios, televisions, and phones, our journey through the history of transistors now takes us to the realm of satellite communication systems. Brace yourself as we dive into the astonishing possibilities that lay ahead in the second half of this chapter.

Satellite communication systems have revolutionized the way we connect across vast distances, enabling global communication and information exchange. The integration of transistors played a vital role in making this technological feat possible.

Transistors have enabled the miniaturization of satellite communication devices, making them lighter, more efficient, and capable of transmitting and receiving signals with remarkable accuracy. By leveraging the properties of transistors, engineers have been able to enhance the performance of satellite communication equipment, making them crucial tools for various industries and everyday communication.

One of the key applications of transistors in satellite communication is in the field of weather forecasting. Weather satellites equipped with advanced transistors gather various data points from Earth's atmosphere, such as temperature, humidity, and cloud formations. These transistors amplify and process these signals, providing meteorologists with invaluable information for accurate weather predictions. Transistors have elevated our understanding of weather patterns, helping us prepare for severe storms, hurricanes, and other natural disasters.

Transistors also play a fundamental role in global positioning systems (GPS). GPS satellites, orbiting our planet, rely on transistors to receive signals from GPS receivers on the ground and transmit precise location data. By calculating the distance between multiple satellites, GPS receivers can accurately determine their location anywhere on Earth. Transistors have reduced the size, improved the accuracy, and made GPS devices widely available, transforming navigation and transportation.

Moreover, transistors have played a pivotal role in the development of communication satellites. These satellites form an extensive network in space, facilitating international phone calls, television broadcasts, and internet connectivity. Transistors are utilized in communication satellites to amplify and transmit signals between ground-based stations and receivers, enabling seamless communication across borders. They have made it possible to connect with people in remote areas, revolutionizing information exchange and enabling global connectivity like never before.

In recent years, transistors have also revolutionized the field of internet connectivity through satellite systems. With the integration of transistors, satellites can provide high-speed internet access to areas without traditional terrestrial infrastructure. This has been a game-changer for remote communities, bringing education, healthcare, and economic opportunities to previously underserved regions.

Transistors have paved the way for a more connected world, where information knows no boundaries.

As we've witnessed throughout this chapter, the journey from Jack Kilby's groundbreaking invention to the widespread applications of transistors in communication systems has been nothing short of remarkable. Transistors have enabled us to carry our favorite tunes with transistor radios, enjoy entertainment on sleek televisions, and communicate effortlessly with phones. They have facilitated the development of mobile communication systems, leading to the smartphones we rely on for countless tasks.

The impact of transistors in satellite communication systems has expanded our horizons even further, enabling precise weather forecasting, accurate navigation, seamless global communication, and internet connectivity across the world. Transistors have become the building blocks of our interconnected society.

As technology enthusiasts, let's take a moment to reflect on how transistors have transformed our lives. From the bulky vacuum tubes of the past to the tiny but mighty transistors of today, the evolution of communication systems continues to shape our world in unimaginable ways.

As we conclude our exploration of transistors in communication systems, remember that this is just one chapter in the vast history of technology. Countless innovations and breakthroughs lie ahead, waiting to be unveiled, driven by the ever-evolving potential of transistors.

The future holds exciting possibilities as we continue to push the boundaries of communication systems. Let's embrace these advancements with anticipation and curiosity, trusting that transistors will continue to be at the forefront of our technological journey.

Stay tuned, fellow technology enthusiasts, for even greater marvels await us in the ever-changing landscape of transistors and their impact on our connected world.

CHAPTER 7:
TRANSISTORS
IN COMPUTING

T ransistors have played a crucial role in the evolution of computers, revolutionizing the way we process information and paving the way for the digital age we live in today. From the early mainframes to the advent of personal computers, the development and integration of transistors have been instrumental in propelling computing technology forward.

In the early days of computing, bulky and power-hungry vacuum tubes served as the primary components for electronic switches. These vacuum tubes were not only inefficient but also limited the speed and scalability of computing systems. However, everything changed with the invention of the transistor by Jack Kilby and the subsequent advancements made by companies like Intel.

It was in 1958 when Jack Kilby, an engineer at Texas Instruments, successfully demonstrated the first working integrated circuit (IC), which combined multiple transistors and other components onto a tiny silicon chip. This breakthrough in miniaturization was a defining moment, as it marked the birth of modern computing.

The development of transistors in

computing technology quickly unfolded, allowing for significant improvements in speed, power efficiency, and reliability. Mainframe computers, which were the norm during the 1960s and 1970s, became smaller and more powerful thanks to the integration of transistors. These machines played a vital role in industries such as finance and scientific research, where massive amounts of data processing were required.

As technology advanced, the demand for smaller, more affordable, and accessible computers grew. This led to the emergence of miniaturized computers known as microcomputers, which eventually evolved into personal computers. The transistor's ability to shrink in size while increasing its functionality made it possible for computers to become a common household item.

One of the pivotal moments in the history of transistors in computing came with the release of the Intel 4004 microprocessor in 1971. This single-chip CPU, comprising over 2,000 transistors, marked the birth of the microprocessor revolution. It paved the way for the development of more powerful and versatile personal computers that could handle complex tasks and calculations.

With each passing year, the number of transistors that could be packed onto a single chip increased exponentially. This phenomenon, known as Moore's Law, named after Intel co-founder Gordon Moore, stated that the number of transistors on a chip would double approximately every two years. This allowed for continuous advancements, facilitating the rise of more capable and sophisticated computing devices.

Transistors not only improved the speed and efficiency of computers but also enabled entirely new functionalities. Real-time processing, graphics capabilities, and the birth of the internet were all made possible due to the rapid development and integration of transistors into computing systems.

As computing power increased, the possibilities seemed endless. Personal computers became a common sight, forever changing the way we work, communicate, and even entertain ourselves. However, the story of transistors in computing doesn't end here. The following developments in the field of transistors would alter the course of technology in ways no one could have predicted.

The second half of this chapter will dive deeper into the innovations brought forth by transistors, exploring their impact on artificial intelligence, mobile computing, and the birth of the digital revolution. Brace yourself for the astonishing transformations that lay ahead in the realm of transistors.

(At this point, we will pause and leave

the readers eagerly waiting for the second half of the chapter, where we will uncover the exciting possibilities and future of transistors in computing.)The second half of this chapter will delve into the remarkable innovations brought forth by transistors, exploring their profound impact on artificial intelligence, mobile computing, and the birth of the digital revolution. Brace yourself for the astonishing transformations that have reshaped the realm of transistors in computing.

Artificial intelligence (AI) encompasses the development of computer systems capable of performing tasks that would typically require human intelligence. Transistors have been instrumental in advancing AI capabilities, enabling the processing power required for complex algorithms and data analysis. As the number of transistors on a chip continued to increase, so did the computational power necessary for AI applications.

The integration of transistors paved the way for significant advancements in machine learning, a subset of AI that focuses on developing algorithms to enable computers to learn from and make predictions or decisions based on data. With the advancements in transistor technology, computers became capable of processing vast amounts of data, extracting patterns, and making informed decisions with remarkable accuracy.

Another significant contribution of transistors in AI was the development of neural networks, which simulate the structure and functionality of the human brain. These networks, composed of interconnected artificial neurons, rely on the massive parallel processing capabilities of transistors to train and recognize patterns in data. Neural networks have revolutionized various fields, from computer vision and natural language processing to speech recognition and autonomous systems.

In parallel with AI advancements, transistors also played a crucial role in the mobile computing revolution. The ever-shrinking size of transistors made it possible to incorporate powerful computing capabilities into portable devices such as smartphones and tablets. This miniaturization allowed for the creation of devices that could perform tasks previously reserved for desktop computers in a compact and convenient form.

Transistors enabled mobile devices to handle extensive processing demands, support high-definition graphics, and connect wirelessly to the internet. This revolutionized the way we communicate, work, and access information, with mobile applications and services becoming an integral part of our daily lives. Transistors have enabled mobile devices to become essential tools in today's world, supporting functions like social media, navigation, and digital assistants.

Furthermore, transistors fueled the birth of the digital revolution by enabling the creation and widespread adoption of digital electronics. Digital technology relies on transistors to process and store information as binary digits, or bits, representing either a 0 or a 1. These two states form the basis of digital information processing, allowing for error correction, precise calculations, and reliable storage.

The integration of transistors on a chip led to the development of digital systems with increased speed, accuracy, and reliability. Digital electronics revolutionized various industries, from telecommunications and entertainment to healthcare and transportation. It facilitated the emergence of high-speed internet connections, media streaming services, digital imaging technologies, and sophisticated medical devices, among many other revolutionary applications.

As we reflect on the remarkable journey transistors have taken in the realm of computing, it becomes clear that their impact goes far beyond the realms of technology enthusiasts. They have reshaped our world, empowering us to achieve feats once unimaginable, connecting us in ways that transcend distance, and fueling the rapid advancement of society as a whole.

In conclusion, the development and integration of transistors have been instrumental in revolutionizing computing technology. They started as a revolution in miniaturization, allowing computers to become smaller, more powerful, and accessible. Transistors facilitated significant advancements in computing power, speed, and reliability, enabling the rise of artificial intelligence and mobile computing. Furthermore, they fueled the digital revolution, transforming various industries and shaping the way we live, work, and interact with the world. The unparalleled potential of transistors continues to drive innovations and shape the future of computing, promising remarkable possibilities that lie ahead.

CHAPTER 8: TRANSISTOR IMPACT ON CONSUMER ELECTRONICS

T hese tiny but mighty components, which replaced bulky and unreliable vacuum tubes in the mid-20th century, revolutionized the way we interact with and experience technology. From calculators to gaming consoles and audio players, transistors have shaped the devices that have become an integral part of our lives.

One of the earliest consumer electronics to benefit from the transistor's impact was the calculator. Prior to transistors, calculators were large and expensive machines, reserved for specialized fields such as engineering and finance. However, with the transistor's compact size, low power consumption, and reliable performance, calculators became more accessible to the general public. Companies like Texas Instruments and Hewlett-Packard played pivotal roles in introducing transistor-based calculators to the market, making complex computations more portable and convenient than ever before.

As the transistor technology advanced, so did its influence on gaming consoles. The birth of home video game systems can be attributed to the integration of transistors into gaming hardware. Before this breakthrough, gaming was largely confined to arcades and specialized venues. However, the advent of transistors allowed for the creation of smaller and more affordable gaming consoles that could be enjoyed in the comfort of one's own home.

The impact of transistors on gaming consoles reached a significant milestone with the introduction of the first programmable video game system: the Fairchild Channel F. Launched in 1976, this iconic console utilized microprocessors and solid-state memory, setting the stage for a new era of interactive entertainment. Subsequent advancements in transistor technology led to the development of iconic gaming consoles such as the Nintendo Entertainment System, Sega Genesis, and PlayStation consoles, which shaped the gaming industry as we know it today.

Transistors didn't just revolutionize gaming; they also transformed the way we listen to and experience music. The birth of portable audio players owes much to the advancements in transistor technology. The invention of the transistor radio in the 1950s marked a turning point in the way people consumed music. With its portable and battery-powered design, the transistor radio enabled music lovers to carry their favorite tunes wherever they went.

As transistors continued to improve, so too did audio players. The cassette player, which enjoyed immense popularity in the 1980s, relied heavily on transistors for its functionality. Compact and portable, these devices allowed music enthusiasts to create personalized playlists and enjoy their favorite songs on the go. Later iterations of audio players, such as portable CD players and eventually MP3 players, further exemplified the lasting impact of transistors on the consumer electronics landscape.

Beyond calculators, gaming consoles, and audio players, the influence of transistors on consumer electronics is vast and far-reaching. From televisions and digital cameras to smartphones and smart home devices, transistors continue to shape the devices we rely on daily. These tiny yet powerful components have enabled ever-increasing functionality, portability, and convenience, transforming the way we live, work, and play.

Let's now explore the specific advancements and breakthroughs that have been shaped by transistors in consumer electronics. From the groundbreaking developments in chip design to the evolution of software and user interfaces, the story of how transistors have revolutionized our devices is both intricate and fascinating.

And with that, the stage is set for the second half of the chapter, where we will unravel the intricate tales and innovations that have further solidified the bond between transistors and consumer electronics. Get ready for an in-depth exploration in the upcoming chapter, where the narrative unfolds and the impact intensifies.In the ever-evolving world of consumer electronics, few advancements have had a more profound influence than the development of transistors. These tiny but mighty components, which replaced bulky and unreliable vacuum tubes in the mid-20th century, revolutionized the way we interact with and experience technology. From calculators to gaming consoles and audio players, transistors have shaped the devices that have become an integral part of our lives.

Transistors have had a significant impact on the development of televisions, transforming them from bulky and unreliable devices to sleek, reliable, and accessible models. Before transistors, television sets relied on vacuum tubes, making them cumbersome and prone to breakdowns. However, with the advent of transistors, TVs became sleeker, more reliable, and accessible to the masses. These advancements allowed for the introduction of smaller and more affordable televisions, leading to increased viewership and the popularization of the medium. Over the years, transistors have continued to play a crucial role in the development of flat-screen displays, high-definition resolution, and smart TV capabilities, enhancing our viewing experience and transforming the way we consume visual content.

Digital cameras also owe their existence and evolution to transistors. Before transistors, cameras relied on film and complex mechanical systems, limiting their accessibility and usability. However, with the invention of image sensors and the incorporation of transistors, digital cameras emerged, ushering in a new era of photography. Transistors enable the conversion of light into digital signals, allowing for instant image capture and processing. This breakthrough revolutionized the photography industry, making cameras smaller, more versatile, and capable of producing high-quality images. Today, digital cameras continue to evolve, thanks to the continuous advancements in transistor technology, enabling us to capture and share our memories with unprecedented ease and clarity.

As transistors became more sophisticated, they found their way into smartphones, arguably one of the most transformative consumer electronics of our time. The integration of transistors into mobile devices revolutionized the way we communicate, access information, and interact with the world around us. Transistors enabled the miniaturization of components, making smartphones compact and powerful. Additionally, they facilitated the development of touchscreens, enabling intuitive and seamless interactions with our devices. With the advent of app stores and mobile internet connectivity, smartphones have become an indispensable tool, encompassing features such as cameras, music players, GPS navigation, and much more. Transistors have been instrumental in driving the rapid evolution of smartphones, fueling innovation and transforming the way we live and connect.

Smart home devices represent yet another area where transistors continue to leave their mark. The integration of transistors into everyday household appliances and gadgets has given rise to a new era of home automation and convenience.

From smart thermostats and security systems to voice-activated assistants and intelligent lighting, transistors enable these devices to communicate, process data, and respond to our needs. Transistors act as the backbone of the interconnected ecosystem that allows us to control and monitor our homes remotely, making our lives more comfortable, efficient, and secure.

In conclusion, transistors have had an immeasurable impact on consumer electronics, shaping and enhancing devices across various categories. From calculators and gaming consoles to televisions, cameras, smartphones, and smart home devices, transistors have been the driving force behind the evolution and advancement of these technologies. Their continuous miniaturization, improved performance, and increased efficiency have paved the way for ever-more sophisticated devices that have become an integral part of our daily lives.

As we delve deeper into the intricate tales and innovations that have further solidified the bond between transistors and consumer electronics, we uncover the limitless possibilities that lie within this realm. The impact of transistors extends far beyond what we can currently fathom, and it is in this exploration that we truly come to appreciate the profound role these tiny components play in shaping our technological landscape.

So, let us continue this journey together, as we unravel the untold stories and remarkable contributions that transistors have made to the world of consumer electronics. Brace yourselves for the discoveries that await us in the second half of this chapter, where we will witness the extraordinary power of these small yet mighty components in action.

CHAPTER 9: TRANSISTORS AND THE SPACE AGE

In the vast realm of technological advancements, few inventions have had as profound an impact as the transistor. From its humble beginnings with Jack Kilby to its subsequent development at Intel, the transistor has revolutionized the world of electronics. In this chapter, we delve into the fascinating ways in which transistors facilitated space exploration, making monumental contributions to satellite technology, space probes, and manned missions.

The dawn of the Space Age ushered in a new era of human exploration beyond the confines of our home planet. As mankind set its sights on the stars, transistors emerged as a crucial technological cornerstone, paving the way for groundbreaking discoveries and achievements. These miniature electronic devices, consisting of semiconducting materials, acted as amplifiers or switches, enabling the control and manipulation of electrical signals. With their compact size and superior performance, transistors were ideally suited for the demanding requirements of space missions.

One of the key areas where transistors played a pivotal role was in satellite technology. Satellites, with their ability to orbit the Earth and relay vital information across vast distances, transformed the way we communicate, observe our planet, and gather data about the universe. Transistors became integral components in satellite communication systems, enabling the efficient transmission and reception of signals. They facilitated the miniaturization of electronics, allowing satellites to accommodate a wide range of instruments and sensors. Consequently, our understanding of Earth's climate, weather patterns, and geological phenomena improved dramatically.

Furthermore, transistors revolutionized the field of space probes, enabling us to explore distant planets, moons, asteroids, and comets. Prior to their invention, space probes were large, cumbersome, and consumed immense amounts of power. However, the integration of transistors into these probes brought about a paradigm shift. Their reduced size and power consumption allowed for more efficient space missions, as the limited resources available during long interplanetary journeys were conserved. Transistors facilitated the recording and processing of scientific data, aiding in the discovery of new celestial bodies, geological formations, and even signs of extraterrestrial life.

Perhaps the most awe-inspiring application of transistors in the space realm was their role in manned missions. Transistors not only enhanced the performance and reliability of spacecraft but also played a crucial part in life support systems. They controlled vital functions such as temperature regulation, oxygen levels, and telemetry data monitoring. As astronauts embarked on perilous journeys to the Moon and beyond, transistors served as the backbone of their technology, ensuring their safety and survival in the harsh conditions of space.

As we reflect upon the history of transistors and their association with the Space Age, it becomes evident that these tiny devices were the unsung heroes behind some of humanity's greatest achievements. They propelled us to new heights, enabling us to explore the cosmos and unlock the mysteries of our universe.

What discoveries and revelations awaited mankind as the transistor revolutionized space exploration? How did this unassuming device continue to shape the trajectory of our quest for knowledge beyond our planet? Stay tuned for the second part of this chapter, where we delve deeper into the fascinating interplay between transistors and the Space Age. Embark on a quest to unveil the mysteries hidden within the cosmos, waiting to reveal their secrets.

(End of first half of the chapter)The second half of the chapter explores the continued impact of transistors on space exploration, delving into their role in navigation systems, scientific experiments, and the communication between Earth and spacecraft.

Space missions rely heavily on accurate navigation systems to ensure precise positioning and trajectory calculations. Transistors have played a crucial role in the development of these systems, enabling the creation of compact yet powerful onboard computers that can efficiently process vast amounts of data. These computers, equipped with advanced transistor technology, have revolutionized spacecraft navigation, allowing for precise course corrections, rendezvous with other celestial bodies, and safe landings on distant worlds.

In addition to navigation, transistors have been a driving force behind scientific experiments conducted in space. They provide scientists with the tools necessary to measure and analyze various phenomena, allowing for groundbreaking discoveries and advancements in our understanding of the universe. Transistors enabled the development of sophisticated instruments, such as spectrometers and cameras, that can capture high-resolution images and detect the presence of different elements and compounds in space. These scientific instruments, powered by transistors, have provided invaluable insights into the composition, dynamics, and evolution of celestial objects, furthering our knowledge of the cosmos.

Communication between Earth and spacecraft has always been of paramount importance in space exploration. Transistors have revolutionized the way we transmit and receive signals across vast distances, ensuring reliable and efficient communication between astronauts and mission control. With the advent of transistors, communication equipment could be miniaturized, reducing the size and weight of spacecraft while maintaining reliable data transmission. Transistors enabled the development of highly sensitive receivers capable of picking up faint signals from deep space, allowing us to gather vital information from the far reaches of the universe. This breakthrough in communication technology also facilitated real-time communication during manned missions, providing astronauts with a vital lifeline to Earth and ensuring their safety and well-being.

As space exploration continues to push boundaries, transistors are poised to play an even more significant role in the future. The development of advanced transistor technologies, such as nanoscale and quantum transistors, holds the promise of further miniaturization, increased processing power, and improved energy efficiency. These advancements will enable spacecraft to carry more sophisticated instruments, increase data transmission speeds, and explore more distant and challenging regions of space.

Beyond that, transistors may even be key to enabling human colonization of other planets. The efficient regulation of life support systems, such as air filtration, temperature control, and waste management, heavily relies on the reliable performance of transistors. Their integration into these systems ensures the health and well-being of future astronauts, making long-duration space missions and eventual settlement on other celestial bodies a possibility.

In conclusion, transistors have been indispensable in propelling space exploration to new frontiers. From their contributions to satellite technology, space probes, and manned missions, to their vital role in navigation systems, scientific experiments, and communication with Earth, transistors have continuously revolutionized the field of space exploration. Their ability to amplify and switch electrical signals, coupled with their compact size and superior performance, have made them ideal for the demanding and often extreme conditions of space. As we stand on the cusp of a new era in space exploration, with ambitions of reaching Mars and beyond, transistors will undoubtedly continue to shape the trajectory of our quest for knowledge beyond our planet. The cosmos holds an infinite number of secrets, waiting for us to uncover them, and with the aid of transistors, our journey towards unraveling those mysteries can only accelerate.

CHAPTER 10: TRANSISTOR-BASED MEDICAL INNOVATIONS

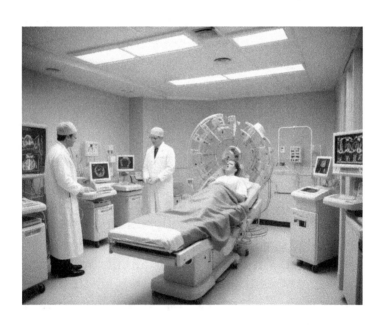

T hroughout history, the field of medicine has been constantly evolving and pushing the boundaries of what is possible. From ancient medicinal practices to modern technological advancements, the quest to improve healthcare has always been at the forefront of human progress. In this chapter, we delve into the profound impact and transformative role that transistors have played in medical innovations.

Transistors, tiny electronic devices that control the flow of electrical current, have revolutionized the field of medicine in countless ways. Developed by the brilliant engineer Jack Kilby and later incorporated by companies like Intel, transistors have paved the way for groundbreaking advancements in diagnostic equipment, prosthetics, and life-saving devices.

One of the most significant areas in which transistors have made a lasting impact is in the development of diagnostic equipment. In the past, medical professionals relied on cumbersome and time-consuming methods to diagnose illnesses and assess patient conditions. However, with the integration of transistors into medical devices, the process has become faster, more precise, and non-invasive.

For instance, transistors have revolutionized imaging technologies such as X-ray machines, magnetic resonance imaging (MRI) scanners, and computed tomography (CT) scanners. By harnessing the power and versatility of transistors, these devices can now produce high-resolution images of the human body, allowing doctors to identify conditions with unprecedented accuracy. This improvement in diagnostic capabilities has led to earlier detection and more effective treatment of various diseases and medical conditions.

Moreover, the utilization of transistors in monitoring devices has greatly enhanced patient care. From portable heart monitors to continuous glucose monitoring systems, these devices rely on transistors to accurately measure vital signs and provide real-time data to healthcare providers. This wealth of information enables doctors to make more informed decisions, proactively intervene in emergencies, and create personalized treatment plans tailored to individual patients.

In the realm of prosthetics, transistors have played an instrumental role in restoring mobility and improving the quality of life for individuals with limb loss or impairment. Prosthetic limbs equipped with transistors and sensors can now replicate the complex movements and functionalities of natural limbs, allowing users to perform daily activities more easily and with greater precision.

Gone are the days of passive prosthetics; the integration of transistors enables these devices to interpret signals from the brain or remaining muscles, translating them into intricate movements. This breakthrough has not only restored physical capabilities but has also had a profound impact on the psychological well-being of individuals, empowering them to regain their independence.

Transistors have also been instrumental in the development of life-saving medical devices. From pacemakers to defibrillators, these tiny electronic components ensure the proper functioning of these devices, enabling them to deliver critical interventions that can mean the difference between life and death. By accurately sensing the electrical impulses of the heart and precisely controlling therapeutic interventions, transistors have transformed cardiac care and extended the lives of millions.

Furthermore, transistors have opened new frontiers in the realm of minimally invasive surgery. Through the use of specialized instruments equipped with tiny transistors, surgeons can perform intricate procedures with greater precision and minimal damage to surrounding tissues. This has led to shorter recovery times, reduced complications, and improved patient outcomes.

As we have explored some of the remarkable advancements facilitated by transistors in the field of medicine, it is evident that these tiny devices have had a profound impact on healthcare. From enhancing diagnostic capabilities to revolutionizing prosthetics and life-saving devices, transistors continue to shape and reshape the landscape of medical innovations.

The second half of this chapter will delve even further into the exciting developments in the field of transistor-based medical innovations. The journey has only just begun, and the future holds boundless possibilities for the intersection of technology and healthcare.Transistors continue to drive innovation in medical advancements beyond the explored advancements in the first half of this chapter. In this second half, we will delve even further into the exciting developments in the field of transistor-based medical innovations. Prepare to be fascinated by the potential of smart medical devices, personalized medicine, and the integration of artificial intelligence.

One of the most promising areas in which transistors are making significant strides is in the realm of smart medical devices. These devices, equipped with transistors and interconnected sensors, have the ability to collect real-time data about a patient's vital signs, activity levels, and other important health metrics. By continuously monitoring these parameters, smart medical devices can detect early warning signs of potential health issues, allowing for proactive interventions and personalized care.

For instance, wearable devices such as smartwatches and fitness bands, powered by transistors, have gained popularity among individuals seeking to monitor their overall health and well-being. These devices can track heart rate, sleep patterns, and physical activity, providing users with valuable insights into their health and helping them make informed decisions about their lifestyle choices.

Furthermore, transistors are enabling the development of implantable medical devices that have revolutionized healthcare. One remarkable example is the pacemaker, a life-saving device that relies on transistors to regulate and correct irregular heart rhythms. These miniature electronic components sense the electrical impulses of the heart and introduce appropriate interventions to maintain a healthy heartbeat.

Moreover, transistors are instrumental in the development of insulin pumps for individuals with diabetes. These devices continuously measure blood glucose levels and administer insulin accordingly, enhancing the management of this chronic condition and improving the quality of life for millions of patients.

Beyond the realm of smart medical devices, transistors have also played a significant role in advancing personalized medicine. With the integration of transistors, medical professionals can now tailor treatment plans to individual patients, taking into account their unique genetic makeup and physiological characteristics.

Genetic sequencing, one of the diagnostic techniques revolutionized by transistors, allows medical professionals to analyze an individual's DNA and identify genetic mutations or predispositions to certain diseases. This knowledge enables personalized treatment plans and the development of targeted therapies that are more effective and have fewer side effects.

Additionally, transistors have facilitated the development of personalized drug delivery systems. Microchips equipped with transistors can be inserted into the body to release medications at precise intervals, ensuring optimal therapeutic levels without the need for constant monitoring or manual administration. This approach has the potential to revolutionize the treatment of chronic conditions such as cancer, where a continuous and controlled release of medication is crucial for success.

The integration of artificial intelligence (AI) has further amplified the potential of transistors in the field of medicine. AI algorithms can analyze vast amounts of medical data, including patient records, diagnostic images, and research studies, to identify patterns, make accurate diagnoses, and even predict treatment outcomes.

For example, with the aid of AI and transistors, radiologists can enhance their workflow and improve the accuracy of their interpretations. AI algorithms can quickly analyze medical images and highlight areas of concern, reducing the time it takes to diagnose conditions like cancer, and allowing for earlier interventions.

Furthermore, the combination of AI, transistors, and robotics has paved the way for revolutionary advancements in surgical procedures. Surgical robots equipped with transistors and AI algorithms can assist surgeons in performing complex procedures with greater precision and control, minimizing human error and improving patient outcomes. These advancements have the potential to democratize surgical expertise and make critical interventions accessible to a wider population.

As we reach the end of this chapter, it is evident that the journey from Jack Kilby to Intel has not only shaped the history of transistors but has transformed the field of medicine in unimaginable ways. Transistors have had an extraordinary impact on healthcare innovations, ranging from diagnostics to personalized medicine and AI integration.

It is with great excitement and anticipation that we move forward, exploring the endless possibilities that lie ahead in the intersection of technology and healthcare. The future brims with endless possibilities, driven by the passion and ingenuity of technology enthusiasts like you, shaping the trajectory of medical innovations powered by transistors.

CHAPTER 11: TRANSISTORS AND THE AUTOMOTIVE INDUSTRY

W hen it comes to the integration of transistors in automobiles, we can witness a remarkable advancement that has revolutionized the world of transportation. The automotive industry has consistently embraced technological innovations to enhance vehicle safety, efficiency, and introduce advanced features, and the implementation of transistors has played a crucial role in achieving these goals.

Transistors, as electronic devices that regulate the flow of electrical currents, have become an integral component within modern automobiles. Gone are the days when mechanical systems dominated the automotive landscape. Transistors have paved the way for sophisticated electronic systems that have transformed the driving experience.

One key area where transistors have made a significant impact in the automotive industry is vehicle safety. With the introduction of electronic stability control (ESC) systems, transistors have played a pivotal role in preventing accidents and improving the overall safety of vehicles. ESC systems utilize transistors to monitor various sensors, including wheel speed, steering angle, and acceleration, enabling the system to detect and prevent loss of control situations by selectively applying brakes or adjusting engine power.

Moreover, transistors have also played a vital role in the development of advanced driver assistance systems (ADAS). These systems rely on transistors to process and analyze data from sensors such as cameras, radar, and LIDAR, allowing vehicles to detect potential hazards and provide warnings to the driver. Transistors have played a crucial role in enabling safety features like lane departure warning systems and adaptive cruise control, contributing significantly to automotive safety.

Beyond safety, transistors have contributed

to enhancing the efficiency of vehicles. The integration of transistors in engine management systems has resulted in improved fuel efficiency and reduced emissions. By precisely controlling fuel injection, ignition timing, and other parameters, transistors optimize the combustion process, leading to better fuel economy and lower environmental impact.

Another area where transistors have transformed the automotive industry is in the realm of advanced features and entertainment systems. From infotainment systems to navigation units, transistors have made it possible for drivers and passengers to access a myriad of functionalities at their fingertips. Transistors enable the processing power required to deliver real-time traffic information, connect to smartphones, and provide multimedia entertainment options.

Furthermore, the integration of transistors has also facilitated the development of electric and hybrid vehicles. Transistors are at the heart of the power electronics systems that convert and regulate electrical energy in these vehicles. Their ability to handle high-power switching operations efficiently has allowed for the proliferation of electric and hybrid models, paving the way for a greener and more sustainable future in the automotive industry.

As we delve deeper into the integration

of transistors in automobiles, it becomes clear that their impact reaches far beyond the realms of safety, efficiency, and advanced features. Transistors have set the stage for the next generation of autonomous vehicles. The ability of transistors to process vast amounts of data with high speed and accuracy is crucial for autonomous driving systems that rely on complex algorithms and artificial intelligence.

In the second half of this chapter, we will examine the advancements in autonomous driving technology and the role transistors play in bringing us closer to a future where vehicles can navigate and operate without human intervention.

...

An essential aspect of the integration of transistors in automobiles is the advancement of autonomous driving technology. As we move towards a future where vehicles can navigate and operate without human intervention, transistors play a critical role in making this vision a reality.

Autonomous driving systems rely on complex algorithms and artificial intelligence to process vast amounts of data and make real-time decisions. Transistors, with their ability to process information with high speed and accuracy, provide the necessary computational power for these systems.

One of the key challenges in autonomous driving is sensor fusion, where data from various sensors such as cameras, radars, and LIDARs needs to be combined and analyzed. Transistors enable the integration and processing of this sensor data, allowing autonomous vehicles to perceive their surroundings accurately.

Transistors also play a crucial role in decision making and control processes. As vehicles navigate through complex traffic scenarios, transistors enable the analysis of real-time data to make informed decisions, such as when to change lanes or how to respond to unexpected obstacles.

Furthermore, transistors are at the heart of the communication and connectivity systems in autonomous vehicles. Through advanced transistors, vehicles can exchange information with each other and with infrastructure, enabling improved coordination and cooperation on the roads. This connectivity also extends to cloud-based services, where transistors facilitate the transmission and processing of data that can further enhance the capabilities of autonomous driving systems.

The integration of transistors in autonomous vehicles not only improves safety but also offers new possibilities for mobility. With autonomous driving, vehicles can be shared, leading to a more efficient use of resources and reducing the number of vehicles on the road.

Transistors enable the seamless coordination of these shared mobility services, ensuring optimal utilization and a smoother overall transportation experience.

The role of transistors in the development of autonomous driving technology will continue to be increasingly significant as we explore and advance in this field. Advancements in transistor technology, including the development of smaller and more energy-efficient transistors, will enhance the capabilities and performance of autonomous vehicles, making them more efficient and reliable.

However, the journey towards fully autonomous vehicles is not without challenges. There are still regulatory, ethical, and technological hurdles to overcome. Transistors will continue to play a vital role in ensuring the safety and reliability of autonomous driving systems, emphasizing their ongoing importance in this critical aspect.

The integration of transistors in automobiles has revolutionized the industry, enhancing safety, efficiency, and introducing advanced features. From electronic stability control systems to advanced driver assistance systems, transistors have significantly contributed to improving the safety of vehicles on the road. Additionally, their implementation in engine management systems has led to greater fuel efficiency and reduced emissions.

Transistors have also played a pivotal role in the development of advanced features and entertainment systems, providing drivers and passengers with a multitude of functionalities and conveniences. Furthermore, the integration of transistors has enabled the rise of electric and hybrid vehicles, paving the way for a greener and more sustainable future in transportation.

As we delve deeper into the integration of transistors in automobiles, it becomes evident that their impact extends far beyond the realms of safety, efficiency, and advanced features. In the second half of this chapter, we have explored how transistors not only contribute to autonomous driving technology but also serve as the building blocks for a future where vehicles can navigate and operate without human intervention.

As technology enthusiasts, we can look forward to further advancements in transistor technology and the continued integration of transistors in automobiles. As history has demonstrated, the potential of transistors to revolutionize the automotive industry once again is boundless.

CHAPTER 12:
THE FUTURE OF
TRANSISTORS

The history of transistors, from the groundbreaking invention by Jack Kilby to the rise of Intel, is a testament to the immense progress that has been achieved in the world of technology. However, what lies ahead is even more exhilarating.

One area of fascinating research in transistor technology revolves around developing smaller and more efficient devices. Over the years, transistors have steadily decreased in size, leading to the development of microprocessors that can fit millions, if not billions, of transistors onto a single chip. This trend, known as Moore's Law, has been a driving force behind the exponential growth in computing power. However, we are rapidly approaching physical limits on how small traditional transistors can become.

To overcome this challenge, scientists and engineers are exploring alternative materials and structures that could potentially replace traditional silicon-based transistors. One such material that has captured significant attention is graphene. Graphene is a single layer of carbon atoms arranged in a flat lattice, known for its exceptional properties that make it a great choice for future transistors. Graphene transistors could potentially offer superior performance, including faster switching speeds and lower power consumption, paving the way for the next generation of electronic devices.

Another promising avenue of research is the development of quantum transistors. Unlike traditional transistors, which rely on the flow of electrons, quantum transistors harness the unique properties of quantum mechanics. These transistors can take advantage of quantum superposition and entanglement to perform computations at speeds that are unimaginable with classical computers. While quantum transistors are still in the experimental stage, they hold immense potential for revolutionizing fields such as cryptography, drug discovery, and optimization problems.

Furthermore, scientists are exploring innovative ways to overcome the performance limitations imposed by traditional computing architectures. One such approach is neuromorphic computing, which aims to mimic the structure and function of the human brain. By leveraging the principles of neural networks, neuromorphic chips could usher in a new era of artificial intelligence, capable of handling complex tasks with unprecedented efficiency.

In addition to these groundbreaking advancements, nanotechnology continues to play a pivotal role in shaping the future of transistors.

Researchers are exploring ways to manipulate materials at the atomic and molecular level, enabling the fabrication of nanoscale transistors with extraordinary properties. For instance, carbon nanotube transistors have emerged as a viable alternative to traditional silicon-based transistors. These nanotubes possess exceptional electrical properties, including high conductivity and superior thermal performance, making them an attractive option for future electronic devices.

Beyond the realm of traditional solid-state transistors, unconventional technologies are also emerging. For example, spintronics utilizes the spin of electrons to encode and process information, offering the possibility of ultra-low-power and ultra-fast devices. Moreover, researchers are investigating the potential of topological insulators, materials that exhibit unique electronic properties that could enable the creation of more robust and energy-efficient transistors.

Embark on an exciting journey into the realm of technological marvels as we explore the future possibilities of transistors. The potential breakthroughs and emerging technologies discussed in this chapter merely scratch the surface of what lies ahead. The application of transistors in fields such as quantum computing, biotechnology, and energy holds immense promise, and their impact on society will undoubtedly be transformative.

Continuing our exploration, we will delve deeper into these captivating advancements and their transformative implications. The journey of transistors is far from over, and the possibilities that await us are boundless. Join us as we continue this exploration into the realm of the unknown, where the boundaries of technology know no limits.As we delve further into the realm of the future of transistors, it becomes clear that the possibilities for advancements are boundless. In this second half of Chapter 12, we will continue exploring the exciting developments and their implications for technology enthusiasts worldwide.

One area of ongoing research in transistor technology is the development of novel materials with unique properties. For instance, indium gallium arsenide (InGaAs) has gained attention as a potential replacement for traditional silicon transistors in high-speed applications. InGaAs transistors have the ability to operate at higher frequencies, allowing for faster data processing and communication. These advancements could revolutionize fields such as telecommunications, where speed and efficiency are paramount.

Another avenue of exploration is the use of nanowires in transistor design. These incredibly thin wires, often only a few nanometers in diameter, hold immense promise for the future of transistors. Nanowire transistors can be constructed from various materials, such as germanium or III-V compound semiconductors, and offer advantages such as improved control over electron flow and reduced power consumption. Additionally, nanowires can be implemented in three-dimensional transistor architectures, further enhancing their performance and potential applications.

Furthermore, the development of flexible and stretchable transistors opens up new possibilities for electronic devices. These transistors, often composed of organic materials or engineered nanomaterials, can be bent, twisted, and stretched without losing their functionality. This breakthrough paves the way for futuristic devices like wearable electronics, foldable displays, and even electronic skin that can seamlessly integrate with our bodies.

Additionally, the field of photonic transistors holds great promise in enabling ultra-fast and highly efficient data transfer. By harnessing light instead of electrons, photonic transistors can transmit information at incredible speeds while consuming significantly less power. This technology has the potential to revolutionize data centers, telecommunications networks, and even quantum computing, propelling us into an era of faster and more sustainable information processing.

As we continue to explore the future of transistors, it is important to acknowledge the critical role that advancements in manufacturing processes play. Techniques such as atomic layer deposition (ALD), extreme ultraviolet (EUV) lithography, and directed self-assembly (DSA) have already demonstrated their ability to fabricate increasingly smaller and more intricate transistor structures. These manufacturing breakthroughs pave the way for continued progress in transistor technology, enabling the realization of increasingly powerful and energy-efficient devices.

Moreover, the integration of transistors into emerging fields like biotechnology and energy holds immense promise. For instance, transistors can be used to interface with neural structures, allowing for the development of advanced brain-computer interface technologies. This convergence of biotechnology and transistors opens up possibilities for cognitive enhancement, neuroprosthetics, and even mind-controlled devices.

In the realm of energy, transistors play a vital role in renewable energy systems. By improving the efficiency of solar panels and energy storage devices, transistors contribute to a greener future. Furthermore, the advent of energy harvesting transistors has enabled the conversion of waste heat from industrial processes into usable electrical energy, significantly reducing energy waste.

As our exploration into the future of transistors comes to a close, it is evident that the journey is far from over. The rapid pace of technological advancement, fueled by ongoing research and innovative breakthroughs, ensures that the possibilities for transistors remain limitless. The applications of these advancements reach far beyond computing and electronics, influencing diverse fields such as healthcare, communications, transportation, and beyond.

With each new breakthrough, technology enthusiasts are presented with a future that holds unimaginable opportunities. The quest for smaller, more efficient, and versatile transistors pushes the boundaries of our understanding, leading to transformative inventions that redefine what is possible.

As we bid farewell to this chapter, we embrace the uncertainties of the future with excitement, knowing that the journey from Jack Kilby to Intel represents only the beginning of an incredible story. Embrace the unfolding era of transistors, where the extraordinary becomes the ordinary, paving the way for a future beyond imagination.

CHAPTER 13: MATERIALS AND MANUFACTURING TECHNIQUES

T ransistors are the fundamental building blocks of modern electronics, and their production has undergone significant advancements since their inception. In this chapter, we will explore various materials and manufacturing techniques employed in transistor production, illustrating their impact on performance and efficiency.

It is essential to consider the materials used in transistor manufacturing, as they directly influence the device's electrical and physical properties. Initially, germanium was the primary semiconductor material used in transistors. Germanium transistors, developed by Jack Kilby and Robert Noyce in the late 1950s, played a crucial role in paving the way for the digital revolution. However, as transistors became smaller and faster, the industry shifted towards using silicon as the preferred semiconductor material.

Silicon possesses several advantages over germanium due to its superior properties. The abundance of silicon in the Earth's crust makes it more cost-effective, and its thermal stability allows transistors to operate at higher temperatures. Furthermore, silicon has a higher bandgap, making it less prone to leakage currents, resulting in improved performance and power efficiency. Today, silicon is the foundation of the vast majority of transistors used in modern electronic devices.

Manufacturing techniques have also evolved significantly to meet the demands of miniaturization and improved performance. One crucial process in transistor production is photolithography, which enables the creation of intricate patterns on the silicon wafer. Photolithography involves using light-sensitive materials called photoresists, which undergo chemical changes when exposed to light. By selectively exposing and developing these photoresists, intricate patterns for transistor components, such as gates and contacts, can be etched onto the silicon wafer.

To further enhance transistor performance, innovative techniques such as ion implantation and epitaxy have emerged. Ion implantation involves bombarding the silicon wafer with ions to alter its electrical properties selectively. This technique allows for precise control over the concentration and distribution of dopants, enhancing the transistor's conductivity and speed. Epitaxy, on the other hand, involves growing a single-crystal silicon layer on the wafer's surface, improving the overall structural integrity of the transistor.

Another critical aspect of transistor manufacturing is the creation of metal interconnects. These interconnects establish electrical connections between transistors and other components, enabling the flow of signals within the integrated circuit. Initially, aluminum was the go-to material for interconnects due to its conductivity properties. However, as transistor density increased, aluminum's resistance to electrical current posed limitations.

To overcome these limitations, the industry transitioned to using copper interconnects. Copper provides lower resistance, higher current-carrying capacity, and improved heat dissipation, making it ideal for today's intricate chip designs. The integration of copper interconnects has significantly contributed to the ever-increasing density and performance of modern transistors.

As we delve deeper into the world of transistors, it becomes evident that materials and manufacturing techniques continue to shape the landscape of electronics. The tireless quest for minuscule, swifter, and eco-friendly devices has sparked revolutionary breakthroughs and revelations. However, the story of materials and manufacturing techniques in transistor production does not end here. In the next part of this chapter, we will uncover cutting-edge advancements and future possibilities, pushing the boundaries of what transistors can achieve.

While we have already witnessed the significant advancements in materials and manufacturing techniques, the journey through the history of transistors continues with more exciting innovations and future possibilities that push the boundaries of what these tiny yet powerful devices can achieve.

One groundbreaking technique that has emerged in recent years is three-dimensional (3D) transistor architecture. As transistors became smaller and smaller, designers faced immense challenges in maintaining performance and efficiency. The traditional planar approach, where transistors are placed side by side on a flat surface, started to show limitations. Enter 3D transistors, also known as FinFETs or tri-gate transistors.

In this innovative design, the transistor is constructed as a fin-like structure standing perpendicular to the silicon substrate, resembling a finfish. This vertical arrangement significantly increases the surface area available for current flow, resulting in improved conductivity and reduced leakage currents. Furthermore, it allows for better control of the transistor's behavior, enabling faster switching speed and lower power consumption compared to their planar counterparts.

3D transistors have played a pivotal role in maintaining Moore's Law, which states that the number of transistors on integrated circuits doubles approximately every two years, facilitating the continuous miniaturization of electronic devices. The implementation of these transistors has enabled the development of more powerful processors, equipped to manage intricate tasks with remarkable speed and efficiency.

As we venture further into the realm of materials and manufacturing techniques, we encounter another remarkable advancement known as nanotechnology. While traditional transistor manufacturing involved working with structures on the microscale, nanotechnology allows for manipulating materials and components on an atomic or molecular scale.

One application of nanotechnology in transistor production is the utilization of carbon nanotubes. These incredibly tiny cylindrical structures, made from rolled-up sheets of graphene, exhibit exceptional electrical and mechanical properties. Carbon nanotube transistors have shown great promise in delivering high-performance devices, exceeding the capabilities of silicon-based transistors.

Researchers are also exploring the potential of alternative materials, such as nanowires and 2D materials like molybdenum disulfide and black phosphorus, to create transistors with unique properties. These materials offer exciting possibilities for achieving unprecedented levels of performance, efficiency, and flexibility in electronic devices.

Advancements in manufacturing techniques have not only focused on improving the performance of transistors but also on enhancing their sustainability. Amid growing environmental concerns, the semiconductor industry has made significant strides in adopting sustainable practices like reducing waste and energy consumption.

One such initiative is the development of environmentally friendly manufacturing processes that minimize the use of hazardous substances. By introducing eco-friendly materials like recyclable plastics and implementing energy-efficient manufacturing processes, the industry aims to reduce its environmental impact while advancing technologically.

Furthermore, it is worth mentioning the increasing emphasis on recycling and reusing electronic waste. The integration of circular economy principles in transistor production allows for the recovery of valuable materials from discarded devices, reducing the strain on natural resources and minimizing electronic waste's impact on the environment.

In conclusion, as the world of transistors evolves, fueled by the relentless pursuit of advancement, consider the transformative potential of smaller, faster, and eco-friendly devices in your own endeavors. Through the exploration of various materials and manufacturing techniques, we have witnessed the transition from germanium to silicon as the preferred semiconductor material, the emergence of innovative processes like photolithography and ion implantation, and the integration of copper interconnects.

But the story doesn't end here. As we delve into the realm of 3D transistors, nanotechnology, alternative materials, and sustainable practices, a world of endless possibilities unfolds before us. The journey through the history of transistors reveals the extraordinary advancements that shape the landscape of electronics, promising a future where technology continues to astound and delight us with its ingenuity.

CHAPTER 14:
TRANSISTOR
SCALING
LIMITATIONS

Transistors are the building blocks of modern electronics, revolutionizing the world of technology since their invention by Jack Kilby. Over the years, these tiny devices have undergone significant transformations, shrinking in size and increasing in performance. However, as technology continues to advance and transistors approach nanoscale dimensions, they face a formidable challenge - the limitations in scaling.

Understanding the challenges associated with scaling transistors down to nanoscale dimensions is crucial for any technology enthusiast. Such knowledge helps in comprehending the complexities involved in maintaining Moore's Law and the potential solutions proposed to overcome these hurdles.

One of the primary limitations faced in transistor scaling is the phenomenon of quantum tunneling. Transistors operate by controlling the flow of electrons through a channel. In traditional transistors, a gate electrode regulates this flow by forming a barrier that either allows or restricts the passage of electrons. However, as transistors become smaller, the thickness of the barrier decreases, leading to electron leakage through quantum tunneling. This results in an unwanted current flow even when the transistor is supposed to be off, leading to increased power consumption and reduced device performance.

To address the issue of quantum tunneling, researchers have proposed multiple solutions. One promising approach is the utilization of new materials that exhibit higher electron confinement. For instance, transition metal dichalcogenides such as molybdenum disulfide (MoS2) and tungsten diselenide (WSe2) have shown promise in achieving better control over electron transport, even at nanoscale dimensions. By using these materials, researchers hope to curb the phenomenon of quantum tunneling and enhance the performance of scaled-down transistors.

Another significant limitation in transistor scaling relates to the onset of thermal effects. As transistors shrink, the density of electronic components on a chip increases, leading to a higher power density. This concentrated power generates heat, and when not effectively dissipated, it can significantly impact the device's performance and reliability. Excessive heat can cause breakdowns, altering the characteristics of the transistor and rendering it useless.

To combat thermal limitations, novel cooling techniques have been developed. One such technique is the integration of carbon nanotubes as efficient heat sinks. Carbon nanotubes possess exceptional thermal conductivity, allowing them to efficiently dissipate heat generated by nanoscale transistors. Additionally, innovative chip packaging designs incorporating microfluidic cooling systems and advanced thermal interface materials have shown potential in managing the rising temperatures in scaled-down devices.

Furthermore, the issue of power consumption and energy efficiency arises as transistors reach nanoscale dimensions. Traditional scaling of transistors led to reduced power consumption due to decreased voltage supply. However, as the size shrinks further, leakage currents and power dissipation increase exponentially. In turn, this not only affects battery life but also hinders the operation of portable electronic devices.

Various strategies have been explored to mitigate power consumption and enhance energy efficiency in nanoscale transistors. One method involves the development of low-power transistor architectures and advanced power management techniques. These approaches strive to reduce leakage currents and optimize power distribution within the transistor design, resulting in improved energy efficiency. Another potential solution lies in the utilization of emerging technologies such as spintronics and quantum computing, which offer promising alternatives with higher energy efficiency and reduced power consumption.

As we unravel the challenges faced in scaling transistors down to nanoscale dimensions, it becomes evident that potential solutions are on the horizon. Through the exploration of innovative materials, cooling techniques, and energy-efficient transistor designs, researchers are determined to push the boundaries of transistor scaling. The possibilities seem endless, and the advancements yet to come hold the promise of a more efficient and powerful future for technology.

In addition to the challenges mentioned earlier, another limitation encountered in transistor scaling is the issue of variability. As transistors shrink to nanoscale dimensions, the inherent randomness in the behavior and characteristics of individual transistors becomes more pronounced. This variability poses a significant problem in terms of manufacturing and device performance.

In order to address this limitation, researchers have been investigating techniques to improve transistor consistency and reduce variability. One approach involves the utilization of advanced manufacturing processes, such as extreme ultraviolet (EUV) lithography. EUV lithography enables the production of finer and more precise transistor features, which helps to minimize variations in transistor performance.

Moreover, techniques like statistical analysis and machine learning algorithms are being employed to better understand and predict transistor behavior, allowing for the identification and correction of any variations that may arise during the manufacturing process.

Furthermore, transistor scaling also faces challenges in terms of reliability and durability. As transistors shrink, they become more susceptible to phenomena like hot carrier injection, electromigration, and oxide breakdown. These issues can cause the deterioration of a transistor's performance over time, leading to reduced device reliability and lifespan.

To overcome these reliability limitations, materials and design improvements are being pursued. For instance, the introduction of high-k dielectrics and metal gates as replacements for traditional silicon dioxide gate oxides has shown promise in mitigating hot carrier effects and improving transistor performance. Additionally, advancements in transistor architectures, such as FinFETs and nanowires, offer improved control over transistor behavior and enhanced reliability in nanoscale devices.

Alongside reliability concerns, the integration of transistors at nanoscale dimensions also presents challenges in terms of manufacturability and cost-effectiveness. Traditional fabrication techniques struggle to achieve the precision required to produce nanoscale transistors on a mass scale. Additionally, the cost of manufacturing these tiny devices can be prohibitively expensive.

To tackle these challenges, novel manufacturing approaches are being explored. Techniques like directed self-assembly and nanoimprint lithography show promise in achieving the necessary precision for large-scale production of nanoscale transistors at reduced costs. Furthermore, advancements in materials and processes, such as the utilization of self-aligned double patterning and 3D integration, enable the development of more cost-effective transistor technologies while maintaining high performance.

As the limitations of transistor scaling continue to be addressed, it is worth noting that researchers are also exploring alternatives to traditional transistor technologies. Novel concepts like tunneling field-effect transistors (TFETs) and memristors offer potential solutions to overcome the scaling limitations faced in traditional MOSFET transistors. These alternative technologies leverage different physical mechanisms and materials to achieve enhanced performance and improved energy efficiency.

Moreover, the future of transistor scaling is not limited to just technological advancements, but also requires a collaborative approach involving interdisciplinary research and innovation. Fields such as materials science, physics, chemistry, and engineering need to come together to pioneer new discoveries and breakthroughs in nanoscale transistor technologies.

In conclusion, the scaling limitations faced by transistors as they approach nanoscale dimensions present formidable challenges. From quantum tunneling and thermal effects to power consumption and variability, each limitation requires innovative solutions to enhance transistor performance, reliability, and manufacturability.

Through the application of advanced materials, new manufacturing techniques, and alternative transistor technologies, researchers aim to overcome these limitations and drive the future of technology forward. As technology enthusiasts, understanding these challenges and the potential solutions being explored allows us to appreciate the complexity behind the devices that power our modern world and fuels our anticipation for the remarkable advancements yet to come.

CHAPTER 15: TRANSISTOR-BASED QUANTUM COMPUTING

I n the vast landscape of technology, few discoveries have had as profound an impact as the transistor. From its humble beginnings with Jack Kilby, who revolutionized the field with the first integrated circuit, to the advancements made by Intel, the journey through the history of transistors is a testament to human innovation and progress. As we delve into the realm of quantum computing, we witness the harmonious fusion of transistors and quantum mechanics, paving the way for a truly transformative technology.

Quantum computing represents a paradigm shift from classical computing, harnessing the unique properties of quantum mechanics to perform calculations with unparalleled speed and efficiency. At the heart of this revolutionary technology lies transistors, acting as the building blocks of quantum circuits. These quantum bits, or qubits, are the fundamental units of information in quantum computing, and their manipulation relies on the intricate control provided by transistors.

Traditional computing relies on binary digits, or bits, which can hold a value of either 0 or 1. Qubits, on the other hand, can exist in a superposition of both 0 and 1 simultaneously, opening doors to exponentially greater computational power. This ability to exist in multiple states concurrently is what sets quantum computing apart and holds immense potential for solving complex problems that would be practically impossible for classical computers.

To understand how transistors enable quantum computing, we must first comprehend the foundational principles of quantum mechanics. Transistors operate based on the concept of electron flow, where electric current is controlled through the manipulation of electron movement. In quantum computing, however, qubits are formed by leveraging quantum phenomena such as superposition and entanglement.

Superposition allows qubits to exist in a state of multiple probabilities simultaneously. This phenomenon is akin to a coin that is both heads and tails at the same time, until observed or measured. In the context of transistors, this superposition is achieved through precise control of electron flow and the use of quantum gates, which manipulate the quantum state of the qubits.

Entanglement, another peculiar property of quantum mechanics, is what truly sets quantum computing apart. When qubits are entangled, their states become interconnected, regardless of the physical distance between them. A change in the state of one qubit immediately affects the state of its entangled counterpart, enabling incredibly powerful computational capabilities. Transistors provide the necessary control and manipulation required to create and utilize entangled qubits, further advancing the potential of quantum computing.

While the promise of quantum computing is incredibly enticing, there are numerous challenges to overcome. One of the major hurdles lies in maintaining the delicate quantum state of qubits, which is easily disrupted by external factors such as temperature or electromagnetic interference. Transistors play a critical role in the design of quantum circuits, allowing for precise control and protection of qubits to mitigate these challenges.

As researchers and engineers continue to push the boundaries of what is possible in quantum computing, the role of transistors becomes increasingly significant. By refining transistor fabrication techniques and exploring novel materials, such as superconductors and topological insulators, scientists aim to create more efficient and reliable qubits that can withstand environmental disturbances.

The potential applications of quantum computing are vast and diverse. From optimizing complex supply chains and simulating chemical reactions to advancing artificial intelligence and cryptography, the impact on various industries is poised to be revolutionary. As we dive deeper into the realm of quantum computing, the second half of this chapter will explore specific use cases and the ongoing efforts to harness the full power of transistors and quantum mechanics.

But for now, let us pause and reflect on the remarkable fusion of transistors and quantum mechanics that has brought us to this moment. The transition from Jack Kilby's monumental breakthrough to the pioneering strides of Intel and beyond has not only set but also elevated the stage for a transformative era in computing. The possibilities are limitless, and the future holds exciting discoveries that may reshape our world as we know it. Stay tuned as we venture into the uncharted territories of quantum computing, and prepare to witness the transformative power of transistors in action.

Within the realm of quantum computing, the seamless integration of transistors and quantum mechanics has paved the way for a truly transformative technology. As we continue our journey through this fascinating field, let us explore the specific use cases and ongoing efforts to harness the full power of transistors and quantum mechanics.

One of the most promising applications of quantum computing lies in optimization problems. Complex supply chains, transportation routes, and logistics networks can be incredibly challenging to optimize efficiently. However, with quantum computing, these problems can be approached in novel ways, allowing for improved resource allocation, reduced costs, and increased overall efficiency. Industries such as manufacturing, healthcare, and finance stand to benefit greatly from these advancements, streamlining their operations and improving their bottom line.

Another area where the potential of quantum computing shines brightly is in simulating chemical reactions. The behavior of molecules, particularly at the quantum level, is incredibly complex and difficult to model accurately. Traditional computing methods struggle to provide precise simulations for larger molecules due to the exponential increase in computational complexity. Quantum computers, on the other hand, possess the inherent ability to handle such calculations efficiently, opening doors to advances in drug discovery, material design, and renewable energy research.

Artificial intelligence (AI) is yet another field poised for significant disruption by quantum computing. The training of AI models can be an immensely resource-intensive task, often requiring weeks or months to complete on classical hardware. Quantum computers have the potential to drastically reduce the time needed for model training by leveraging their parallel computational capabilities. This could enable more rapid development and deployment of AI technologies, leading to breakthroughs in areas such as natural language processing, image recognition, and autonomous systems.

Cryptography, the practice of secure communication, is expected to experience a revolution with the advent of quantum computers. While classical computers utilize algorithms that are mathematically difficult to reverse engineer, their cryptographic security could be easily compromised by a large-scale quantum computer. Quantum computing, on the other hand, offers the potential to develop new cryptographic techniques that are resistant to attacks from both classical and quantum computers. This has led to extensive research into post-quantum cryptography, ensuring that our digital infrastructure remains secure in the face of future advancements.

As the potential of quantum computing becomes clearer, researchers and engineers continue to dedicate their efforts to overcome the numerous challenges on the path to practical implementation. One of the primary hurdles lies in error correction and fault tolerance. Quantum bits, or qubits, are highly susceptible to errors caused by environmental disturbances. To counteract these errors, scientists are actively investigating methods for error correction and developing fault-tolerant quantum systems. Transistors play a vital role in mitigating errors, allowing for the maximum precision and control required for error correction protocols.

Furthermore, the scalability of quantum computing remains a significant challenge. While quantum processors with a small number of qubits have been realized, scaling these systems to the size required for practical applications poses a significant engineering hurdle. Transistors, serving as the essential building blocks of quantum circuits, play a crucial role in scaling up quantum processors. Advances in transistor fabrication techniques and the exploration of novel materials hold the key to achieving larger, more complex quantum systems.

As we conclude this dive into the world of transistor-based quantum computing, it is essential to acknowledge the remarkable fusion of transistors and quantum mechanics that has brought us to this juncture. The journey from Jack Kilby's groundbreaking integrated circuit to the present day has propelled us into a new era of computing—a realm full of limitless possibilities.

While challenges remain, the ongoing efforts of researchers, engineers, and technology enthusiasts alike inspire optimism. Quantum computing has the potential to revolutionize industries ranging from healthcare to finance, from cryptography to AI. As we unveil the transformative power of transistors in action, the future holds the promise of groundbreaking discoveries that may reshape our world as we know it.

Let us continue to delve further into uncharted territories, exploring the untapped potential of quantum computing and the pivotal role of transistors. Together, we stand at the forefront of a technological revolution that will redefine the limits of human innovation and progress. Prepare to embark on a journey through uncharted territories as we unlock new frontiers and embrace the transformative power of transistor-based quantum computing.

CHAPTER 16:
TRANSISTORS
AND RENEWABLE
ENERGY

R enewable energy technologies have revolutionized the way we generate and utilize power. Solar panels, wind turbines, and smart grids have become increasingly common solutions in our pursuit of sustainability. Behind the scenes of these technologies lies a vital component that has played a significant role in their development and efficiency: transistors.

Transistors, which are tiny electronic components that regulate the movement of electricity, have played a crucial role in advancing renewable energy technologies. Their capacity to strengthen and redirect electrical signals has facilitated progress in generating, storing, and transmitting power. Let's explore the fascinating intersection of transistors and renewable energy.

Solar panels harness the abundant energy emitted by the sun and convert it into electricity. These photovoltaic devices rely on transistors to manage the flow of energy within the system. In the heart of solar panels, transistors act as electronic switches that help optimize the conversion of sunlight into usable power. By redirecting the flow of electrons and ensuring the efficient operation of each solar cell, transistors contribute to maximizing the energy output of these panels.

The integration of transistors in solar panels has also led to the development of innovative technologies such as microinverters. Microinverters, small electronic devices connected to each solar panel, convert the direct current (DC) produced by the panels into alternating current (AC) that can be used to power homes or feed back into the grid. Transistors are essential in converting solar energy by managing the flow and alteration of electrical signals, which enhances the efficiency of solar energy systems.

Moving forward, wind turbines have emerged as another pivotal player in the renewable energy landscape. As wind passes through their rotating blades, these turbines generate mechanical energy that is converted into electrical energy using high-tech systems. Transistors play an instrumental role in these systems by controlling and enhancing the flow of electricity at various stages.

In wind turbine generators, transistors are utilized in power converters that adjust the voltage and frequency of the produced electricity, ensuring its compatibility with the grid. By effectively managing the transformation and transmission of electrical energy, transistors allow wind turbines to generate consistent power with maximum efficiency. Additionally, transistors also assist in monitoring wind turbine performance, enabling real-time adjustments to optimize power generation and facilitate maintenance.

Beyond direct power generation, transistors find their place in the realm of smart grids. Smart grids are intelligent electrical grids that leverage advanced technology to efficiently manage power supply and demand. These grids rely on transistors for numerous functions, from monitoring and controlling power flow to optimizing energy usage.

Transistors enable smart grids to intelligently distribute electricity, adapting to fluctuating demand and balancing the power flow between renewable energy sources and traditional power plants. Through robust monitoring systems, transistors provide real-time data on power consumption, allowing for more accurate load forecasting and efficient energy distribution. By actively facilitating the incorporation of renewable energy sources into the grid, transistors help transform the power sector into a more sustainable and reliable network.

In conclusion, transistors have brought about a paradigm shift in renewable energy technologies. From solar panels to wind turbines and smart grids, these electronic components have significantly contributed to the growth and efficiency of clean energy solutions. Through their ability to control and amplify electronic signals, transistors have enabled the optimization of power generation, storage, and distribution systems. Delving further into the second half of this chapter, you will uncover the future potential and exciting developments awaiting at the intersection of transistors and renewable energy.

Continuing our journey through the captivating intersection of transistors and renewable energy, we unveil further exciting developments and future potential.

One area where transistors have made a remarkable impact is in the realm of energy storage systems. As renewable energy sources such as solar and wind are intermittent by nature, efficient and reliable storage solutions are crucial to ensure a consistent power supply. Transistors play a critical role in the control and optimization of energy storage systems, such as batteries and capacitors.

In battery technology, transistors help regulate the charging and discharging processes, ensuring that energy flows efficiently between the battery cells and the devices they power. Transistors enable precise control of current flow, voltage levels, and temperature, which not only enhances the overall performance of batteries but also extends their lifespan. With advancements in transistor technology, we can anticipate further improvements in the efficiency and capacity of energy storage systems, paving the way for a more reliable and sustainable energy future.

Moreover, capacitors, as energy storage devices with the ability to deliver short bursts of power, also benefit greatly from transistor integration. Transistors enable the precise control of charge and discharge rates, allowing capacitors to store and release energy efficiently. This has implications in renewable energy systems where rapid response and energy delivery are important, such as in stabilizing the output of solar and wind power plants during fluctuating conditions. Transistors facilitate the seamless integration of capacitors into renewable energy systems, enabling enhanced energy management on a broader scale.

Transistors are at the forefront of innovation in creating energy-saving and smart appliances. With the rise of smart homes and the Internet of Things (IoT), transistors play a pivotal role in optimizing energy usage and enabling communication between devices.

By integrating transistors into appliances such as refrigerators, heating systems, and lighting fixtures, these devices can intelligently adjust energy consumption based on real-time data. This not only reduces energy waste but also contributes to overall energy efficiency and cost savings. Transistors act as the electronic brain, analyzing data and making decisions to optimize energy usage, ultimately creating a more sustainable and interconnected environment.

Furthermore, the integration of transistors in energy management systems has paved the way for more effective demand response strategies. Demand response refers to the ability to adjust electricity usage in response to supply and demand conditions. Transistors enable intelligent monitoring and control systems that can communicate with appliances and devices to synchronize energy consumption with periods of lower demand or higher availability of renewable energy.

This capability not only helps prevent blackouts and overloading of the electrical grid but also ensures a more balanced distribution of energy resources. By incentivizing users to shift their energy consumption to off-peak hours or times when renewable energy production is high, transistors facilitate the integration of clean energy sources into the existing grid infrastructure, reducing reliance on fossil fuel-based power plants.

In conclusion, as we look towards the future, the role of transistors in renewable energy technologies continues to expand and evolve. These small electronic devices have revolutionized the way we generate, store, and consume power. From enhancing the efficiency of solar panels and wind turbines to enabling energy storage systems and powering intelligent appliances, transistors have become indispensable in our pursuit of a sustainable energy future.

With ongoing advancements in transistor technology and the increasing integration of renewable energy into our daily lives, the possibilities are endless. As technology enthusiasts, let us embrace the potential that lies at the nexus of transistors and renewable energy, knowing that our collective efforts can create a cleaner and more sustainable world for generations to come.

CHAPTER 17:
TRANSISTORS
IN WEARABLE
TECHNOLOGY

P icture a scenario where your watch not only displays the time but also monitors your physical activity, heart rate, and enables communication with others. Or envision a pair of glasses that overlays digital information onto the real world, opening up a whole new realm of possibilities. Thanks to the remarkable integration of transistors, wearable technology has become a reality, revolutionizing the way we interact with devices and the world around us.

As previously discussed, transistors are the fundamental components of modern electronic devices. These tiny semiconductor devices are instrumental in amplifying and switching electrical signals, enabling the creation of complex circuits that form the backbone of all electronic devices. Transistors have been instrumental in shaping our contemporary digital world, from computers to smartphones. And now, they have found their way into the world of wearable technology.

One significant area where transistors have made a transformative impact is in smartwatches. These stylish timepieces have come a long way from their humble origins, evolving into powerful miniature computers that sit comfortably on our wrists. Within these sleek and compact designs, transistors enable a range of functionalities that make our lives more convenient and interconnected than ever before.

At the heart of every smartwatch lies a microprocessor, a complex network of transistors that serves as the brain of the device. This miniaturized version of traditional computer processors enables the smartwatch to perform a multitude of tasks, from displaying notifications to running apps and tracking fitness metrics. The integration of transistors allows these devices to process information quickly and efficiently, providing us with real-time updates on our health, schedule, and other important aspects of our lives.

Fitness trackers, another category of wearable technology, owe their existence to the remarkable advancements in transistor integration. These devices, typically worn on the wrist or attached to clothing, are designed to monitor physical activity, heart rate, and sleep patterns, among other health-related metrics. By employing specialized sensors and a network of transistors, fitness trackers can gather and process data to provide users with valuable insights into their overall well-being.

Augmented reality (AR) glasses represent another groundbreaking application of transistors in the realm of wearable technology. These futuristic glasses are capable of overlaying digital information onto the wearer's field of vision, seamlessly blending the virtual and real worlds. The integration of transistors enables AR glasses to handle the complex computational tasks required to track and analyze the surrounding environment, thus enhancing our perception and interaction with the world.

Whether it's the convenience of a smartwatch, the insights offered by a fitness tracker, or the immersive experiences of augmented reality glasses, the integration of transistors in wearable technology has opened up a myriad of possibilities. However, this is just the beginning of a fascinating journey that lies ahead. As technology continues to advance at an unprecedented pace, we can expect even more innovative use cases for transistors in wearables.

In the second half of this chapter, we will delve deeper into the future of transistors in wearable technology. We will explore cutting-edge developments, such as flexible and stretchable transistors, that promise to redefine the very nature of wearables. We will also discuss the challenges and opportunities that lie ahead as we strive to create devices that seamlessly merge with our everyday lives. Get ready to embark on a thrilling exploration of the next frontier in wearable technology, where transistors are poised to redefine our relationship with the digital world.

The future is full of possibilities, just

waiting to be explored and embraced. But for now, we leave you with tantalizing thoughts of what lies ahead. Transistors have brought us this far, and they will undoubtedly shape the future of wearable technology. Get ready for the upcoming chapter, where we will uncover the thrilling developments in the realm of transistors in wearables.

While the integration of transistors in wearable technology has already made significant strides in enhancing our daily lives, the future of this technology holds even more exciting developments. In the second half of this chapter, we will dive further into the promising advancements that lie ahead and the challenges and opportunities they present.

One of the most thrilling prospects on the horizon is the emergence of flexible and stretchable transistors. Traditional transistors are rigid and inflexible, posing limitations on the design and form factor of wearable devices. However, researchers have been experimenting with new materials and fabrication techniques to create transistors that can bend and stretch without losing functionality.

Imagine a smartwatch or fitness tracker that seamlessly wraps around your wrist like a second skin, conforming to your movements and providing a more natural and comfortable user experience. With flexible and stretchable transistors, wearables could become even more integrated into our daily routines and seamlessly adapt to our needs.

These advancements in transistor technology also hold great potential for healthcare applications. Flexible transistors could be integrated into wearable patches or clothing, enabling continuous health monitoring and disease management. Such devices could revolutionize remote patient monitoring, allowing healthcare professionals to gather real-time data on their patients' vitals and well-being, while individuals can take better control of their own health.

Another area of exploration in the future of transistors in wearables is energy harvesting. As wearables become more embedded in our lives, the need for convenient and sustainable power sources becomes increasingly crucial. Transistors could play a vital role in converting the surrounding energy, such as body heat or motion, into usable electrical power. This breakthrough could potentially eliminate the need for frequent charging or cumbersome batteries, making wearables even more practical and user-friendly.

Additionally, the integration of transistors in wearables opens up opportunities for enhanced human-computer interaction. Imagine controlling your wearable device simply by moving your fingers or eyes, thanks to integrated touch or gaze sensors powered by transistors. This could revolutionize the way we interact with wearable technology, making it more intuitive and seamless.

While the future of transistors in wearables holds immense promise, it also comes with its fair share of challenges. As technology continues to advance, there is a constant push for more powerful and energy-efficient transistors. Researchers are exploring new materials, such as graphene and carbon nanotubes, that could potentially outperform conventional silicon transistors and pave the way for even more efficient and compact wearables.

However, the integration of these new materials into mass production remains a hurdle. Ensuring their reliability, scalability, and cost-effectiveness on a large scale requires extensive research and development.

Furthermore, as wearable devices become more pervasive, concerns around data privacy and security increase. The vast amount of personal data collected by wearables, such as health metrics and location information, calls for robust encryption and protection mechanisms. Transistors, in combination with advanced encryption techniques, are crucial for safeguarding individual's privacy and maintaining the integrity of wearable technology.

In conclusion, the integration of transistors

in wearable technology has opened up a world of possibilities, revolutionizing the way we interact with devices and the world around us. From smartwatches and fitness trackers to augmented reality glasses, transistors have become the building blocks of these innovative devices, providing efficient processing power and enabling a range of functionalities.

Looking ahead, the future of transistors in wearables holds tremendous potential for advancements in flexible and stretchable technologies, energy harvesting, improved human-computer interaction, and healthcare applications. However, researchers and industry leaders must overcome challenges such as developing new materials, ensuring reliability, and addressing privacy concerns to unlock these opportunities fully.

As technology enthusiasts, it is an exciting time to witness the transformation and evolution of wearable technology. The journey is far from over, and the possibilities are endless. Prepare for the upcoming chapter, where we will uncover yet another captivating facet of technological advancements shaping our world.

CHAPTER 18: TRANSISTORS AND ARTIFICIAL INTELLIGENCE

T he rapid advancement of technology has paved the way for countless breakthroughs and innovations over the years. From the invention of the first electronic computer by Jack Kilby to the birth of Intel, the history of transistors is intricately intertwined with the development of artificial intelligence (AI). In this chapter, we will explore the fascinating intersection of transistors and AI, delving into their mutual impact and the future implications for both fields.

Transistors, originally developed as electronic switches in the mid-20th century, revolutionized the world of computing. These tiny semiconductor devices acted as amplifiers, signal processors, and switches in electronic circuits, enabling the miniaturization of electronic devices and ultimately leading to the creation of the modern computer. The invention of the transistor by Jack Kilby and his colleagues at Texas Instruments in 1958 laid the foundation for the technological advancements that followed.

As transistors became smaller, faster, and more efficient, they paved the way for the development of AI. Artificial intelligence, a field of computer science dedicated to creating intelligent machines and systems, relies heavily on the processing power provided by transistors. The exponential growth of computational capabilities made possible by advancements in transistor technology significantly accelerated progress in AI research.

One of the key areas where transistors have fueled advancements in AI is the field of machine learning. Machine learning algorithms enable computers to learn from data and make predictions or decisions without being explicitly programmed. This data-centric approach is made possible by the availability of high-performance transistors, which can process large datasets and perform complex calculations in real-time.

The marriage of transistors and AI has led to numerous practical applications. From autonomous vehicles to voice assistants, AI-driven technologies have become ubiquitous in our daily lives. Transistors play a vital role as the processing backbone of these AI systems, allowing them to analyze vast amounts of data, recognize patterns, and make informed decisions.

However, the relationship between transistors and AI is not limited to one-sided benefits. As AI continues to evolve, it has also started influencing advancements in transistor technology. The demand for more powerful AI systems has driven the development of specialized transistors designed to meet the computational requirements of AI algorithms. These specialized transistors, such as graphics processing units (GPUs) and tensor processing units (TPUs), are optimized for the complex calculations required in AI applications.

Looking towards the future, the intersection of transistors and AI holds immense potential. The ongoing progress in AI research, coupled with advancements in transistor technology, promises to revolutionize various industries. From healthcare to finance, AI-powered systems have the potential to transform how we approach complex problems and make informed decisions.

However, as we delve deeper into the integration of transistors and AI, ethical concerns arise. The rapid development of AI technology poses challenges regarding privacy, security, and the potential impact on the job market. These concerns call for careful examination and responsible development of AI systems, ensuring that the benefits are maximized while minimizing potential risks.

With the first half of the chapter now completed, we have only scratched the surface of the intricate relationship between transistors and artificial intelligence. In the second half, we will further explore the implications of this convergence, discussing the exciting prospects of neuromorphic computing, the ethical dilemmas surrounding AI development, and the potential for truly intelligent machines.

Get ready for the next part of our journey exploring the history of transistors and artificial intelligence, where we delve deeper into the implications and potential of this transformative intersection.

As we continue our exploration of the fascinating intersection of transistors and artificial intelligence, we delve deeper into the implications and potential of this transformative convergence.

One exciting prospect that arises from this convergence is the development of neuromorphic computing. Neuromorphic systems aim to replicate the structure and functionality of the human brain, using specialized hardware and algorithms inspired by neural networks. By leveraging the power of transistors, these systems can simulate complex brain-like processes and enable the development of more efficient and intelligent machines.

Neuromorphic computing holds immense promise for a wide range of applications. For example, in the field of robotics, neuromorphic systems can enhance autonomous navigation and perception capabilities. By mimicking the brain's ability to process sensory inputs and make real-time decisions, robots can navigate complex environments with greater efficiency and adaptability.

Additionally, neuromorphic computing can revolutionize the field of healthcare. By harnessing the power of transistors and AI, researchers can develop advanced diagnostic tools capable of analyzing vast amounts of medical data and accurately predicting disease progression. These intelligent systems can aid doctors in making more precise and personalized treatment plans, leading to improved patient outcomes.

However, as we embrace the potential of neuromorphic computing and AI, ethical dilemmas arise. The development of intelligent machines raises concerns about privacy, security, and the impact on the job market. It is crucial that we approach AI development with responsible consideration, ensuring that the benefits are maximized while minimizing potential risks.

The ethical implications of AI extend beyond privacy and job displacement. The algorithms that power AI systems are designed and trained by humans, and these algorithms can inadvertently perpetuate biases and reinforce existing societal inequalities. To address this issue, it is essential to promote diversity and inclusivity in AI research and development, ensuring that the technology is developed with a broad range of perspectives and ethical guidelines.

Another aspect to consider is the integration of AI with human decision-making. As AI systems become more capable and autonomous, the question of accountability arises. How do we ensure that AI systems make ethical decisions aligned with human values? It is crucial to establish frameworks and regulations that govern the use and deployment of AI, promoting transparency, accountability, and fairness.

Furthermore, the potential for truly intelligent machines opens up exciting possibilities in various industries. From finance to transportation, AI-powered systems can revolutionize how we approach complex problems and make informed decisions. Imagine a future where financial institutions leverage AI algorithms to predict market trends accurately and make investment recommendations. Or a transportation system that optimizes traffic flow and reduces congestion through an interconnected network of AI-controlled vehicles.

In addition to these practical applications, the integration of transistors and AI also holds potential for scientific advancements. AI systems can assist researchers in analyzing vast amounts of data, leading to new insights and breakthroughs in fields like genomics, material science, and climate modeling. By leveraging the computational capabilities of transistors, AI accelerates the pace of scientific discovery, opening up new frontiers of knowledge.

As we wrap up our exploration of the intricate relationship between transistors and artificial intelligence, the future brims with excitement and boundless possibilities. Both fields continue to drive each other's advancements, with transistors enabling the processing power required for AI, and AI pushing the boundaries of transistor technology.

As technology enthusiasts, we have a responsibility to stay informed and actively participate in shaping the future of transistors and AI. By engaging in discussions, advocating for ethical practices, and supporting responsible development, we can ensure that this convergence maximizes its potential for the betterment of society.

The exploration of the history of transistors and artificial intelligence has been nothing short of remarkable. We have witnessed how transistors revolutionized the world of computing, enabling the birth of AI. We have explored the practical applications and potential implications of this convergence while acknowledging the ethical considerations that come with it.

In this chapter, we have only scratched the surface of the intricate relationship between transistors and AI. With ongoing advancements and research, the future is brimming with exciting discoveries and endless possibilities.

As technology continues to evolve, it is certain that the dynamic interplay between transistors and AI will shape the world we live in. Get ready to eagerly anticipate what the future holds, embracing the transformative power of this convergence to unlock the full potential of transistors and artificial intelligence.

CHAPTER 19:
TRANSISTORS
IN ROBOTICS

T ransistors, the tiny electronic devices that revolutionized the world of electronics, have played a significant role in the advancement of robotics and the creation of autonomous machines capable of complex tasks. The marriage of transistors and robotics has led to remarkable developments and pushed the boundaries of what is possible in the field of technology. In this chapter, we will examine how transistors have contributed to the evolution of robotics, allowing machines to become more intelligent, adaptable, and proficient at performing intricate operations.

To truly appreciate the impact of transistors on robotics, we must first delve into the fundamental function of these electronic components. A transistor is essentially a switch that can control the flow of current in an electronic circuit. By regulating the flow of electricity, transistors enable computers and other electronic devices to process and manipulate data, effectively functioning as the building blocks of modern technology. It is this ability to control and amplify signals that makes transistors so indispensable in the world of robotics.

One of the key areas where transistors

have profoundly impacted robotics is in the realm of artificial intelligence (AI). Transistors have made it possible to create robotic systems that can analyze vast amounts of data, learn from their environment, and make autonomous decisions based on this acquired knowledge. These intelligent robots rely on the computing power provided by transistors to process complex algorithms and execute tasks with precision and accuracy.

The development of autonomous robots capable of performing intricate tasks has been made feasible due to transistors. These robots, equipped with a multitude of sensors and actuators, are empowered to perceive their surroundings, gather data, and analyze it for decision-making. Transistors enable these robots to process the sensor data in real-time, allowing them to navigate through complex environments, recognize objects, and make autonomous adjustments to achieve their objectives.

One remarkable application of transistors in robotics is in the field of medical surgery. Robotic surgical systems, such as the da Vinci Surgical System, rely heavily on transistors to ensure precise control and manipulation of surgical instruments. By incorporating transistors into the system's control circuitry and amplification units, surgeons can remotely control the robotic arms with exceptional precision. The use of transistors in these surgical robots has revolutionized the medical field, enabling less invasive procedures, improved surgical outcomes, and reduced recovery times for patients.

Moreover, Incorporating transistors into robotics has facilitated progress in industrial automation. Transistors are essential components in the control systems of manufacturing robots, allowing for precise and efficient operation in assembly lines. With the help of transistors, robots can be programmed to perform intricate tasks repeatedly and flawlessly, significantly improving productivity and reducing human error. This symbiotic relationship between transistors and industrial robots has contributed to the growth of industries worldwide, allowing for increased production rates and enhanced quality control.

In addition to their impact on AI, medicine, and industrial automation, transistors have also shaped the field of autonomous vehicles. The advent of self-driving cars would not have been possible without the integration of transistors into their complex control systems. Transistors provide the computational power necessary to process crucial information from various sensors, such as lidar and radar, allowing the vehicle to make intelligent decisions in real-time. With the aid of transistors, these autonomous vehicles can navigate traffic, avoid obstacles, and ensure passenger safety with a high level of autonomy and accuracy.

As we have seen, transistors have been instrumental in pushing the boundaries of robotics. From the development of intelligent and autonomous systems to advancements in medical surgery, industrial automation, and autonomous vehicles, transistors have revolutionized the capabilities of robots and opened up exciting possibilities for the future. The second half of this chapter will delve deeper into the potential of transistors in robotics, exploring emerging trends and future implications for this dynamic and ever-evolving field. Stay tuned for the next chapter, where we will continue our exploration of the fascinating world of transistors and their impact on robotics.Despite the enormous strides made in robotics with the integration of transistors, there are still several challenges to be addressed in this ever-evolving field. One of the key areas of focus is the development of more efficient and powerful transistor technology.

Over the years, transistors have become smaller and more energy-efficient, paving the way for the creation of increasingly compact and agile robots. However, as the demand for more advanced robotic systems continues to grow, there is a need for transistors that not only provide higher processing power but also consume less energy.

Researchers are actively exploring new

materials and designs to overcome these limitations. A promising research area involves exploring the use of nanoscale transistors. By leveraging the unique properties of nanomaterials, such as carbon nanotubes and graphene, scientists aim to create transistors that are smaller, faster, and more energy-efficient than their traditional silicon counterparts. If successful, this could lead to the development of robots that are even more compact, versatile, and effective in performing complex tasks.

Another critical challenge in the field of robotics is ensuring the safety and reliability of autonomous systems. As robots become increasingly autonomous, the need for robust and fail-safe control systems becomes paramount. Transistors play a vital role in implementing these safety features by enabling precise control and monitoring of robotic components.

One approach to addressing safety concerns is the development of redundant systems that utilize multiple transistors in parallel. By duplicating critical circuitry, robots can continue functioning even in the event of transistor failure. Moreover, the integration of advanced diagnostic capabilities into transistors can enable real-time health monitoring, allowing for proactive maintenance and mitigation of potential failures.

Transistors are also at the forefront of enabling more natural human-robot interaction.

As robots become more integrated into our daily lives, it becomes imperative that they can understand and respond to human instructions and cues effectively. Transistors are key components in the development of advanced machine learning algorithms and natural language processing systems, allowing robots to understand and interpret human speech and gestures.

This advancement in human-robot interaction opens up a wide range of possibilities for robots to assist humans in various domains, such as healthcare, eldercare, and education. For example, transistors enable robots to provide personalized care to patients, assist in rehabilitation exercises, or even act as educational companions for children, helping them learn and grow.

In the future, transistors in robotics offer promising opportunities for further development. As the field of robotics continues to progress, there is a growing focus on developing robots that can exhibit emotions and empathy. Transistors are integral to the development of emotional intelligence in robots, allowing them to perceive and respond to human emotions through facial recognition, voice analysis, and body language interpretation.

Imagine a future where robots can not only perform complex tasks efficiently but can also understand and empathize with human emotions, providing companionship and support in various aspects of life. With the steady advancement of transistor technology and the integration of cutting-edge artificial intelligence algorithms, this future is not as far-fetched as it may seem.

In summary, transistors have been essential in shaping the field of robotics, allowing the creation of smart, self-operating machines capable of intricate tasks. Transistors have transformed robots, enhancing their abilities and paving the way for exciting future prospects, from AI and medicine to automation and self-driving vehicles.

As technology enthusiasts, we can look forward to witnessing further advancements in transistor technology, as researchers strive to create more powerful, energy-efficient, and reliable transistors for the next generation of robots. With continued progress, robots will continue to challenge our perceptions and push the boundaries of what is possible, revolutionizing the way we interact with technology and the world around us.

CHAPTER 20: ETHICAL CONSIDERATION S AND THE FUTURE OF TRANSISTORS

Transistors have revolutionized the world of technology, enabling the creation of powerful computers, smartphones, and countless electronic devices we rely on daily. However, as with any technological advancement, it is crucial to reflect on the ethical implications that transistor technology brings and consider the potential future advancements that may further impact society.

Privacy is a significant ethical concern related to transistor technology. With the shrinking size and increased efficiency of transistors, they can now store and process large volumes of personal data. While this has led to remarkable developments in fields like artificial intelligence and data analytics, it has also raised concerns about the potential misuse and unauthorized access to sensitive information.

In an increasingly connected world, the ethical responsibility lies with both individuals and organizations to protect user privacy. Striking the balance between leveraging the benefits of transistor technology while safeguarding personal information is a pressing challenge that requires constant vigilance and robust regulatory frameworks.

Another ethical concern involves the digital divide. As transistor technology advances, the digital divide between those who have access to technology and those who do not becomes more pronounced. While developed nations and urban areas enjoy the advantages brought by advancements in transistors, marginalized communities and rural areas may be left behind.

Ensuring equal access to technology and bridging the digital divide is a crucial ethical consideration that needs to be addressed. Efforts must be made to provide affordable and accessible technology, as well as comprehensive digital literacy programs, to empower individuals from all walks of life and prevent further societal inequalities.

Furthermore, the advancement of transistor technology brings with it environmental considerations. The manufacturing process of transistors involves the use of rare earth elements and hazardous chemicals that can have detrimental effects on ecosystems and human health. The disposal of electronic waste containing transistors also poses a significant environmental challenge.

Efforts should be made to develop and implement sustainable manufacturing practices, such as reducing the use of harmful substances and promoting recycling programs. Additionally, exploring alternative materials and methods for transistor production could help mitigate the environmental impact associated with the technology.

Looking towards the future, the potential advancements in transistor technology are boundless. From the development of even smaller and more efficient transistors to the emergence of advanced quantum computing, the landscape of possibilities is vast.

One potential future advancement is the integration of transistors into wearable technology, allowing for seamless connectivity and the monitoring of health conditions. Picture a scenario where your smartwatch not just records your movements but also keeps an eye on your health indicators, notifying you of any health concerns.

Moreover, transistors could play a pivotal role in the advancement of renewable energy technologies. By enhancing the efficiency of solar panels and energy storage devices, transistors could propel the adoption of clean energy sources, mitigating climate change and reducing our dependence on fossil fuels.

The impact of these potential advancements on society cannot be overstated. They hold the promise of improving our lives, empowering individuals, and solving pressing global challenges. However, it is imperative that as these advancements come to fruition, the ethical considerations discussed earlier are prioritized, ensuring a future that is both technologically advanced and ethically sound.

As we embark on the second half of this chapter, we will delve deeper into the potential implications of these advancements and explore the dilemmas and opportunities they present. By examining the ethical considerations surrounding transistor technology and delving into the potential future advancements, we hope to navigate the path forward and shape a future that benefits all of humanity. In the first half of this chapter, we discussed the ethical implications surrounding privacy, the digital divide, and the environment. Let's now explore the potential impact of future advancements in transistor technology and how they may shape society.

One area that shows great promise is the field of medical technology. With ever smaller and more efficient transistors, we can envision an era of personalized medicine. Imagine a world where wearable devices equipped with advanced transistors can continuously monitor our health, detect early signs of disease, and provide personalized treatment recommendations. This integration of transistors into medical devices could greatly improve healthcare outcomes and save countless lives.

However, this advancement also raises ethical concerns. As technology becomes more deeply intertwined with our personal lives, issues of data privacy and security become paramount. As we entrust our most intimate health information to these devices, it is crucial that robust safeguards are in place to protect against unauthorized access and ensure the responsible use of this data. Strong ethical guidelines and regulations must be established to ensure that the benefits of these advancements do not come at the expense of individual privacy.

Another area where transistor technology is poised to make a significant impact is in the realm of transportation. Self-driving cars, for instance, rely heavily on the efficient and reliable processing power provided by transistors. These vehicles have the potential to greatly reduce accidents and traffic congestion, as well as increase accessibility for individuals who are unable to drive themselves. Yet, the extensive use of self-driving cars brings up ethical issues about safety, responsibility, and the effects on transportation jobs.

To address these concerns, comprehensive regulations and rigorous safety standards must be put in place. Additionally, measures should be taken to ensure a smooth transition for workers whose jobs may be disrupted by the introduction of self-driving technology. Ethical considerations surrounding the responsible development and implementation of these advancements are crucial to ensure their long-term positive impact on society.

Moreover, progress in transistor technology can greatly influence education. As transistors become more powerful and affordable, the potential for personalized and immersive learning experiences increases. Virtual reality platforms, enhanced with powerful transistors, could revolutionize the way we teach and learn, offering students the opportunity to explore complex concepts in a dynamic and engaging manner.

However, it is essential to consider the potential consequences of relying too heavily on technology in education. While digital tools can enhance learning experiences, they should not replace the value of human interaction and critical thinking. Striking a balance between leveraging technology and nurturing essential human skills is essential to ensure that the educational landscape of the future is both inclusive and effective.

In the realm of environmental conservation, transistor technology has the potential to drive significant advancements. The integration of transistors into energy-efficient devices and infrastructure could facilitate the transition to a more sustainable future. For instance, smart grids using sophisticated transistors can efficiently manage energy flow and reduce wastage. Similarly, the development of energy storage systems featuring highly efficient transistors could help overcome the intermittent nature of renewable energy sources and accelerate the adoption of clean energy solutions.

Yet, in our pursuit of these advancements, it is imperative to prioritize the environmental impact of transistor manufacturing and the disposal of electronic waste. Efforts to reduce the use of hazardous substances in transistor production and promote recycling programs must continue to minimize the ecological footprint of this technology.

To sum up, the future developments in transistor technology present significant chances for advancement and growth in different fields. Across healthcare, transportation, education, and environmental conservation, the profound impact of these advancements on society cannot be overstated. However, the ethical considerations discussed in the first half of this chapter must remain at the forefront of technological development. By ensuring responsible use, addressing privacy concerns, and mitigating potential negative impacts, we can shape a future that benefits all of humanity. As fans of technology, let's unite to support these ethical considerations and shape a future of transistor technology that combines progress and ethical values.

ABOUT THE AUTHOR

Mark Spencer is a technology enthusiast and historian with a deep passion for the evolution of electronics and their impact on modern society. With a background in engineering and a keen interest in the history of technological innovation, Mark has spent over a decade researching and writing about the transformative power of transistors and semiconductors. He holds a Master's degree in Electrical Engineering from the University of Michigan and has contributed to several leading research projects on the development of microelectronics. Mark has been recognized with multiple industry awards for his insightful contributions to the field of technology history. Through public speaking, advocacy, and his writings, Mark Spencer aims to educate and inspire others to appreciate the profound impact that tiny electronic components have had—and will continue to have —on shaping our world. His work highlights the journey from the earliest inventions to the cutting-edge advancements that define today's digital age, with a focus on how these innovations drive progress across every sector of society.

BOOKS BY THIS AUTHOR

The Holy Grail Of Mathematics: Solving The Riemann Hypothesis

Discover the Secret Codes of the Universe: How Solving the Riemann Hypothesis Unlocks Hidden Realms in Mathematics

Ever felt like the deepest secrets of the universe are locked within equations you could never understand? What if you could not only understand them but also feel the thrill of being on the cusp of one of the greatest mathematical discoveries? In "The Holy Grail of Mathematics," Mark Spencer guides you directly into the enigmatic heart of the Riemann Hypothesis.

Transform Your Understanding of Mathematics

Boldly journey where only the most dedicated mathematicians have dared to tread. With Mark Spencer's lucid explanations, you'll:

Grasp the profound implications of solving the Riemann Hypothesis.

Gain insights into the fascinating link between prime numbers and the fabric of mathematical reality.

Discover the tantalizing connections between the Hypothesis and quantum physics.

Experience the beauty of mathematics through the eyes of a passionate expert.

Experience a Revolution in Your Mathematical Worldview

This is not just another math book; it's a transformative expedition that challenges everything you know about numbers and their patterns. With each page, you'll find yourself deeper in the mathematical maze, equipped with the tools to comprehend and appreciate the complexity and elegance of the universe.

Act Now to Embark on Your Mathematical Adventure

Don't just read about the Riemann Hypothesis; immerse yourself in the quest to solve it. Join Mark Spencer as he reveals the allure of this enduring puzzle and inspires you with the relentless spirit of mathematical exploration. Seize this opportunity to witness the unfolding of mathematical history.

Embrace the Challenge — Explore the Infinite

Click the BUY NOW button and step through the portal into a world where mathematics touches the divine, and every number holds a secret waiting to be unraveled.

Hikikomori: Understanding And Overcoming Social Isolation

Discover what it means to live completely outside society's gaze. "Hikikomori" is not just a cultural condition; it's a deep-seated psychological journey that Mark Spencer brings to life through compelling narrative non-fiction. You will see the world through the eyes of those who have vanished from social scenes to battle with their inner demons.

In this book, you'll learn:

The intricate psychology behind the decision to become a hikikomori.
Personal accounts that paint a vivid picture of the day-to-day challenges and insights of living in self-imposed exile.
The societal pressures in Japan that contribute to this phenomenon, which may resonate with readers globally.
Coping mechanisms that individuals develop to

manage their unique way of life.

The impact on families and society, offering a broader understanding of the condition's ripple effect.

"Hikikomori" is more than a label; it's a reality that thousands face, hidden in plain sight. Mark Spencer's exploration into this hidden world is as educational as it is emotional, providing a platform for empathy and understanding. By engaging with these personal narratives, you gain more than knowledge—you gain a new perspective on what it means to be truly alone in a world that values connectivity above all.

Take this journey with Mark Spencer and understand the silent struggle that echoes in the vacant rooms of Japan's youth. Grab your copy today, and unravel the mystery of the hikikomori.

The Quest For Knowledge: A Profound Examination Of The Top 10 Non-Fiction Books That Will Make You Wiser

Unlock Your Potential with Every Page

Ever wondered how the greatest minds harness their potential and insights to influence and reshape the world? "The Quest for Knowledge: A Profound Examination of the Top 10 Non-Fiction

Books That Will Make You Wiser" offers you a roadmap through ten groundbreaking works that have shaped modern thought and innovation.

In this indispensable guide, you'll explore:

How Yuval Noah Harari decodes the past to predict the future in "Sapiens."
Daniel Kahneman's deep dive into the human psyche with "Thinking, Fast and Slow," illuminating the dual aspects of our cognition.
Jared Diamond's revelation of societal evolution driven by geography in "Guns, Germs, and Steel."
The profound impact of Elizabeth Kolbert's "The Sixth Extinction" on our ecological awareness.
Each chapter is crafted to bring forth key insights and practical wisdom from each book, allowing you to apply these timeless truths to enhance your decision-making, critical thinking, and understanding of complex systems.

Take the First Step Towards Intellectual Empowerment

Don't miss the opportunity to expand your horizons, challenge your preconceptions, and ignite your passion for lifelong learning. Begin your journey today by discovering how these seminal books can revolutionize your view of the world and your place within it.

Act Now – Grab your copy of "The Quest for Knowledge" and transform your intellectual landscape!